PRAISE FOR
RISING ABOVE

Wayne Cordeiro's refreshingly personal insights in *Rising Above* can literally help everyone do just that—rise above the storms and struggles of modern life. Wayne points us to the timeless wisdom of God's Word and the resiliency it offers. He shows us that God's ways are always within the reach of His children.

ARCHIBALD HART, PH.D.
SENIOR PROFESSOR OF PSYCHOLOGY, FULLER THEOLOGICAL SEMINARY

KATHLEEN HART
CHAPLAIN TO STUDENT WIVES

In *Rising Above*, Pastor Wayne Cordeiro lays out an obvious choice: You can either allow the rubble of life to pile on top of you or you can use the pile of rubble to climb your way to a better life. After all, it isn't about what happens to you but what happens in you that really counts. You will be encouraged by Pastor Wayne and by God's Word to rise above whatever life throws at you.

JOHN C. MAXWELL
AUTHOR, *LEADERSHIP 101* AND *RUNNING WITH THE GIANTS*
FOUNDER, THE INJOY GROUP

Wayne writes to help us rise above the rubble of life; he speaks as one who—like you and me—knows what it is to struggle in the midst of it. He stands at the intersection of reality and hope. He never points *too* far ahead but always points in the upward direction.

JOHN ORTBERG

Teaching Pastor, Menlo Park Presbyterian Church
Menlo Park, California

RISING ABOVE

WAYNE CORDEIRO

Regal

From Gospel Light
Ventura, California, U.S.A.

PUBLISHED BY REGAL BOOKS
FROM GOSPEL LIGHT
VENTURA, CALIFORNIA, U.S.A.
Regal PRINTED IN THE U.S.A.

Regal Books is a ministry of Gospel Light, a Christian publisher dedicated to serving the local church. We believe God's vision for Gospel Light is to provide church leaders with biblical, user-friendly materials that will help them evangelize, disciple and minister to children, youth and families.

It is our prayer that this Regal book will help you discover biblical truth for your own life and help you meet the needs of others. May God richly bless you.

For a free catalog of resources from Regal Books/Gospel Light, please call your Christian supplier or contact us at 1-800-4-GOSPEL or www.regalbooks.com.

Library of Congress Cataloging-in-Publication Data
Cordeiro, Wayne.
    Rising above / Wayne Cordeiro.
        p. cm.
    ISBN 0-8307-3632-8
    1. Christian life—Meditations.   I. Title.
    BV4501.3.C684 2004
    248.4—dc22   2004015913

1   2   3   4   5   6   7   8   9   10   /   10   09   08   07   06   05   04

CONTENTS

ACKNOWLEDGMENTS

Because of the LORD's great love we are not consumed, for his
compassions never fail.
LAMENTATIONS 3:22, *NIV*

First of all, I want to thank the Community Care Ministries in Hawaii and its great staff of leaders and volunteers. Mark Hovland and his team have given untiringly of themselves to see people set free. Thank you for committing your lives to those who are so precious to God.

To our Prison Ministry led by Roy Yamamoto, you and your team remind me so much of Jesus as you reach out to the men, women and youth in our correctional facilities. Thank you for showing them that true freedom lies not in what side of the bars they are on, but what side of eternity they view life from. To our LifeChange leaders who have invited the Spirit of God to move so wonderfully in our church, we see the fruit of your labors every week.

And to our Intercessors in New Hope led by Pastor Larry Gillis, we have seen not only victories but also numerous lives transformed because people are praying. Evangelism is simply picking up the spoils of a war already won in prayer.

And to the hundreds of Care Group leaders, thank you for being "steadfast, immovable, always abounding in the work of the Lord, knowing that your toil is not in vain in the Lord" (1 Cor. 15:58).

INTRODUCTION

Our life is God's gift to us. What we make of it is our gift to Him.

No one intentionally chooses a mediocre life, a middle-of-the-road family or a second-rate marriage. Our God is a great God, and since He's created us in His image, He intended us to be a great people!

But what do you do when your walls collapse under the pressure of marauding problems and battering storms? The realities of life strike and you are left standing in the ashes of smoldering relationships and broken dreams.

On September 11, 2001, our country experienced one of the most tragic attacks in her history. The terrorist bombing of the World Trade Center in Manhattan caught the world by surprise.

What took years to erect took only one hour to destroy.

We live in a world in which tragedy can strike at any time—divorce, accident, bankruptcy—obliterating our lives and leaving us at rock bottom. Today, millions of people are digging through the rubble of their own lives, sifting for answers to questions that seem to elude understanding.

Yet there is one thing we can agree upon: We must rebuild! Defeat is not when we are knocked down but when we refuse to get back up. We cannot live our lives beneath the rubble; therefore, we must construct the courage to rebuild.

In the months and years ahead, life will return almost to normal. We'll go back to our lives and routines, and that is good. Even grief recedes with time and grace. But our resolve must not pass.

—PRESIDENT GEORGE W. BUSH, FOLLOWING THE 9/11 TRAGEDY

One of the most popular series ever at New Hope is now in your hands. Scores of people who have become part of our church *ohana* (family) did so because they came to a Sunday service in which God used one of the messages in this book to heal a relationship or a collapsed faith.

This book is twofold: (1) It is a hope that you will find answers to your questions, and (2) it is a prayer that you will seek God in your struggle.

While God promises to heal, you decide how long it takes. It can take a decade or a week. You decide. To help you with your decision, I ask you to take a few minutes to let God counsel you through these pages. And while you do, I will be praying that you

Your greatest chapter in life is the one you are about to embark on!

will find a fresh perspective for the days ahead.

Remember, we're all in this together. You are not meant to travel alone. Your greatest chapter in life is the one you are about to embark on!

"For I know the plans that I have for you," declares the LORD, "plans for welfare and not for calamity to give you a future and a hope."

JEREMIAH 29:11

CHAPTER 1

WHAT DO YOU DO WHEN YOU HIT ROCK BOTTOM?

Have you ever heard God say one thing to you and you did another? Have you ever heard specific instructions from God but ended up doing just the opposite? Let me introduce you to Jonah—an Old Testament minor prophet who almost wasn't one at all!

God called Jonah for a special mission. The people of the city of Nineveh were wicked, but God—the God of second chances—commissioned Jonah to intervene and help them reverse their downward spiral. God recruited Jonah and instructed him:

"Jonah, I want you to go to Nineveh. [Nineveh was a three-day trip inland from where Jonah was at that time.] There, I want you to preach to the people because they are truly wicked. I've got better plans for them than destruction, so tell them to turn back to God!" (see Jon. 1:2).

There was just one catch: Jonah hated the Ninevites! He despised them with a passion. They were known as ferocious, unmerciful warriors who plundered and destroyed villages in their greed to possess more lands. Therefore, instead of obeying God's instructions, Jonah took passage on a ship heading in the opposite direction. Jonah sailed *away* from God's call and journeyed toward a place called Tarshish across the Mediterranean Sea.

Most of the important things in the world have been accomplished by people who have kept on trying when there seemed to be no hope at all.

— DALE CARNEGIE

Now God had two problems on His hands: an unrepentant city and a runaway prophet!

However, a colossal storm slammed into the fugitive's boat, hurling Jonah overboard. To top it off, a large fish—we don't know what kind of fish, but we'll call it a whale—swallowed Jonah whole. What we find next is Jonah tangled in seaweed and desperately treading water in swirling whale bile.

Have you ever felt that way? Have you ever hit bottom with nowhere left to go? You feel completely abandoned, left to fend for yourself. We all go through these dead-ends—times when it seems like there's nowhere to go. At one time or another, in varying degrees, each of us has been or will be named "Jonah."

Yet just as God held onto the Jonah of old, He won't let you go. He is not done with you yet! Read on.

A Strange Way to Bless!

For you first, God raised up His Servant and sent Him to bless you by turning every one of you from your wicked ways (Acts 3:26).

Because of God's love, He will go to extremes to get your attention. God's love is not a Hollywood-type romance, nor is it always soft and poetic. Because of God's love for Jonah, He sent a storm. God does that at times. His program of blessings doesn't always come wrapped in soft velvet. It may be delivered to you via Hurricane Jones!

In God's arsenal of attention grabbers, you'll find everything from irritating people to crowing roosters. He also stocks highway maniacs and nagging family members. But one of God's favorite tools to arrest our attention is a *storm*. It's a strange way to deliver a blessing, but it works. And later on, you'll come to appreciate God's love if you understand God's methods.

> *Storms make trees take deeper roots.*
>
> —CLAUDE MCDONALD

These divine tempests come in various shapes and sizes, so let's categorize them into two genres: correcting storms and perfecting storms.

Correcting Storms

Correcting storms do one thing well: They correct! Simple but effective. These storms usually crop up when you are heading in the wrong direction. When you run from God, you will find yourself facing the storm of *consequences*, the storm of *conscience* or the storm of *complaints*, which pounds you with 20-foot swells. Ask Jonah. He experienced a hurricane season when he headed in the opposite direction.

God sees the end from the beginning. He sees our present actions and our futures as a result of those actions. God knew that if Jonah continued in the direction he was headed, his own actions would bring destruction to himself. Therefore, God divinely intervened to correct Jonah's course.

There will be times when we're headed off to Tarshish and God loves us enough to send a storm. It's not intended to capsize us but to correct us. That way, we'll steer well away from hungry whales.

Perfecting Storms

> After you have suffered for a little while, the God of all grace, who called you to His eternal glory in Christ, will Himself perfect, confirm, strengthen and establish you (1 Pet. 5:10).

Perfecting storms are the most confusing, especially if you've been taught that if you do God's will, you'll never encounter problems. If that were true, then Jesus' life would have been one of ease and leisure. Yet nothing is further from the truth.

Our real blessings often appear to us in the shape of pains, losses and disappointments.

—JOSEPH ADDISON

In Matthew 14, we find the classic story of Peter and the disciples in the midst of a storm. Jesus catches up with them in their attempts to cross the Sea of Galilee, but He chooses a more unconventional route. He decides to walk on the water rather than sail on top of it.

Once I visited Helsinki, Finland, where we had planted a church, in the middle of winter and, being from Hawaii, this made for a painful experience. Even now when I think about it, chills run up my spine. It was one of those days when each sentence spoken hung momentarily in the frigid air like a cartoon caption. That evening I spoke on Matthew 14, expounding on the remarkable miracle of Peter's walking on water.

During the message, a person raised his hand and said, "Walking on the water isn't that big of a miracle. Here in Helsinki, we walk on the water all the time. In fact, in a couple of weeks, we will be able to *drive* on the water!"

In this story, Peter gets out of the boat to walk on the water in the midst of a furious storm. "Seeing the wind" (v. 30), Peter begins to be submerged under the raging white caps because he focuses on the problems. He loses confidence in his choice to follow Jesus out onto the water. The Lord immediately reaches out His hand, pulls him up and simply asks, "Why did you doubt?" (v. 31).

Although we often talk about how Peter failed, you must remember that he had enough faith to walk on the water in the first place. It may have been an *imperfect* faith, but I'm sure it was more faith than you or I would have had. I've been to Israel several times and visited the Sea of Galilee, and I must admit that when no one was looking, I tried it, and all I got was wet!

> *When we are flat on our backs, there is no way to look but up.*
> —ROGER W. BABSON

This kind of storm was different from the one on the Mediterranean. The Galilean storm wasn't there to *correct* Peter's faith; its purpose was to *perfect* it!

There will be times when God corrects you and there will be times when God perfects you. Both can be painful, but God allows them because He loves us and understands that sometimes the only way He can get our attention is to let things get out of our control.

Now back to our friend Jonah.

From the Depths of Sheol

Jonah found himself floundering in a correcting storm deep below the sea. He finally came to his senses and cried out to God from the belly of the whale:

> I called out of my distress to the LORD, and He answered me. I cried for help from the depth of Sheol; You heard my voice (Jon. 2:2).

When Jonah hit rock bottom in his life, he finally turned to God. He cried out to God and God answered. By this time the whale was traveling back toward Nineveh, and God gave His final instructions to the whale: "Go ahead and 'urp' him up on the shore" (see v. 10). *Whoosh!* Up came Jonah. He landed in a soggy heap on the beach.

Adversity is a severe instructor, set over us by One who knows us better than we do ourselves, as He loves us better too.

—EDMUND BURKE

Remember that he had been in the whale's stomach for three days, marinating in gastric juices and toxic bile! He smelled pretty ripe and had bleached-white skin and peroxide-dyed hair. But most important, he had a renewed dedication to the Lord and a clear sense of direction! So he took the three-day journey to Nineveh.

He arrived and walked through the streets saying, "Repent! God told me to proclaim to you repentance, so repent!" And lo and behold, the entire city repented (see Jon. 3). Wouldn't you? I would.

As I was ruminating on this, I could just imagine the scene that day. A messenger bursts breathless into the king's court shouting, "King! King! There is a prophet outside telling us to repent! What should we do?"

"Get a grip," says the king (loose Cordeiro translation, of course). The king continues, "What's his name?"

"I think he said, 'Jonah!' But that's not the whole of it. This guy is spooky! He's as white as a sheet with dried seaweed all over his head. His hair is flaming yellow, and he has a powerful odor that follows him around. It smells like whale barf. What should we do?" The king answers, "We're going to repent; that's what we're going to do!"

So the whole city repented.

What changed this renegade prophet from rejection to reception, from dodgeball to hardball? When Jonah hit rock bottom, God was able to give him direction and teach him life lessons. Don't miss the gem: Jonah's rock-bottom experience not only changed his life, but it also changed eternity for over 100,000 people living in Nineveh.

Jonah was made ready to obey God. Where? In the belly of a whale. His story, much like yours and mine, is that often it isn't until we hit rock bottom that we are ready to change our ways.

Attention Getters and Big Fish

God loves each one of us so much that if we head in the wrong direction, He will intervene. Yet if we won't take His advice, He will allow us to hit rock bottom. When there are no more options, no more side doors and no more shortcuts, *then* our hearts are ready to change. God's optimum will, of course, is that we simply obey. However, when we choose not to, He reverts to His arsenal of attention getters and big fish.

His love will pursue you, so watch for Him, especially when the electricity goes out!

He disciplines us for our good, so that we may share His holiness. All discipline for the moment seems not to be joyful, but sorrowful; yet to those who have been trained by it, afterwards it yields the peaceful fruit of righteousness (Heb. 12:10-11).

When I think back on the greatest growth lessons in my life, I realize that they all have one common denominator: In each one I was caught at the bottom of a valley. Having tumbled down many hills, I've discovered the greatest gems are found on the valley floor.

God's Aggressive Love

Because God can see the end from the beginning, He can see when you've been navigating with a faulty compass. What you hold to be true will be tried and tested. Locker-room advisers and Internet chat-room sages leave you abandoned in times of need. You can be sincerely following what you think is right on your compass, but when your compass is off, even though sincere, you're still off. The end result will be your destruction.

Prosperity is a great teacher; adversity a greater.

—WILLIAM HAZLITT

If you're a builder, you'll have blueprints for every proposed house you plan to work on. But if the blueprint is wrong, it doesn't matter how sincerely you build, the house will be faulty. Sometimes God has to erase the whole plan, redraw it and rebuild. God does not take pleasure in raining on your parade, but if the direction you're heading in will only result in collapse, He will call on Hurricane Jones. Mark my words! Without fail, God's reason will always be that He takes great delight in bringing His promises to pass in your life:

> For I know the plans that I have for you . . . plans for welfare and not for calamity to give you a future and a hope (Jer. 29:11).

Back to the Heart

Sometimes God needs to take you all the way back down to bedrock so that He can rebuild and reshape the very motives of your heart. You will find that the greatest battles will not be fought on foreign seas or on the battlefields of a war-ravaged land. *The greatest battles will be won or lost within the inner chambers of your heart.*

He said, "Take now your son, your only son, whom you love, Isaac, and go to the land of Moriah, and offer him there as a burnt offering on one of the mountains of which I will tell you" (Gen. 22:2).

The ultimate measure of a man is not where he stands in moments of comfort and convenience, but where he stands at times of challenge and controversy.

—DR. MARTIN LUTHER KING, JR.

The Bible tells the touching story of Abraham and his beloved son, Isaac, the promise of Israel and the only hope for a lasting legacy. Abraham loved Isaac more than anything else. He lavished all of his affections on his heir. Although Abraham was a wealthy man, nothing made him feel richer than his son.

One day God asked Abraham to take Isaac to the top of Mount Moriah and sacrifice him as one would a sheep or goat! The Bible doesn't describe the agony and confusion that must have raged through Abraham's aged heart. I cannot imagine the pain that tortured him throughout that painful night as he agonized over God's request.

Father of Our Faith

The Bible gives us a glimpse of why Abraham is called the father of our faith. He didn't run. He didn't curse. He didn't question. In fact, it tells us that "early in the morning" (Gen. 22:3), he saddled his donkey, split wood for the sacrifice and headed toward the mountain with his son.

When they reached the top, Abraham took one last look into the eyes of the one he loved so deeply. Without questioning the Lord, he bound his son to the wood. He drew the knife high into the air and, in order to complete the sacrifice, detached his heart from his cherished treasure.

With a calculated obedience that would relinquish all his hopes and dreams, the knife began its swift descent. There is no greater courage than that which the Scriptures unveil to us at the top of Mount Moriah that fateful day.

As the knife plunged toward its intended target, Abraham's arm froze in midair:

Intense love does not measure, it just gives.

—MOTHER TERESA

Abraham stretched out his hand and took the knife to slay his son. But the angel of the LORD called to him from heaven and said, "Abraham, Abraham!" And he said, "Here I am." He said, "Do not stretch out your hand against the lad, and do nothing to him; for now I know that you fear God, since you have not withheld your son, your only son, from Me" (vv. 10-12).

God didn't really want Isaac; He wanted Abraham's heart! As soon as Abraham's affections had been detached from Isaac and placed back where they belonged, God's refining was complete. "Abraham," the Lord said, "My purpose was to gain your heart, not to take your son. And now that your heart has returned, you may keep your son in addition to all of My promises" (see v. 12).

Back to Bedrock
God wants your heart, not your penance or your self-inflicted depression. He wants your commitment to rebuild your life God's way. He is asking you to follow Him! And sometimes—in order to do that—He has to take you all the way back to bedrock.

Where did Moses get his commission and the strength to follow God? When he was in the desert, after his family and friends had rejected him. When he was ostracized and excommunicated as Pharaoh's right-hand man. Driven into the wilderness, he hit rock bottom. However, we often find God in the desert.

A U-Turn Sign at the Bottom

Sometimes we hit the bottom because of our own doing, like the prodigal son. When he rejected his father, he ended up feeding pigs. When the prodigal son was at rock bottom, *then* he came to his senses (see Luke 15:17). God places the best teachers of life at the bottom. It was in the dirt-lined classroom where the prodigal son decided, "This is what I will do: I will go back to

Always remember that problems contain values that have improvement potential.

—NORMAN VINCENT PEALE

my father" (see v. 18). It was at the bottom where the prodigal son found a U-turn sign, which changed his life.

We all hit rock bottom at some point in our lives. We can yell at people, complain against God or get angry at circumstances. Or we can decide to hear what God has to say. Let's consider the following three options when we hit rock bottom.

1. Cry Out to God

They stumbled and there was *none to help*. Then they *cried out to the LORD* in their trouble; He saved them out of their distresses (Ps. 107:12-13, emphasis added).

This point will sound somewhat elementary, but bear with me. When you find yourself on your back staring at the ceiling, don't start blaming your spouse; don't quit; don't buy a ticket to Tarshish; don't pass "go"; and don't collect $200. Instead, you first need to *cry out to God!*

You'll notice Psalm 107:12 say that sometimes you'll stumble and there will be "none to help." Maybe you'll get mad at people for not being there when you need them. You phone your friends, but they're busy. You call the pastor, and he doesn't return your call. (Of course, this never happens in *our* church!) You finally resort to calling the suicide prevention line, and they put you on hold.

We turn to God for help when our foundations are shaking, only to learn that it is God who is shaking them.

—CHARLES C. WEST

The only One who can save you out of your distress is God. Sometimes God will remove people from earshot in order to wean you from your tendency to rely on others more than you rely on God. God allows this in order "that we would not trust in ourselves, but in God" (2 Cor. 1:9).

It's *okay* to cry out to God. We *need* to cry out to God. Often our tendency is to complain against God and get angry with people. We lick our wounds and hold pity parties. We may even want to end our lives. It seems like the last thing we do is cry out to God. Yet often the problem is not the problem. The problem is not hitting rock bottom. The problem is a hardened heart—a pride that disallows tears, an aversion to brokenness or a refusal to house a contrite heart. Despite the problem, God still invites you to Himself. He is showing you the way to the Kingdom, and the signpost you see may just be a U-turn.

Back to the Basics

> In the days of His flesh, He offered up both prayers and supplications *with loud crying and tears* to the One able to save Him from death (Heb. 5:7, emphasis added).

Did you know that Jesus cried out to God? When people came against Him and He felt He was all alone, Jesus cried out to the Father. People ask, "How could Jesus, who is God, have hit rock bottom and have had to cry out to God?"

Although Jesus was fully God, He was also fully man. The Lord was not immune from hurt. He experienced all the pain of fallen humanity, so when He hit the bottom, He went to His knees.

Jesus knew crying out to the Father was His only hope if He wanted to remain pliable and not succumb to hardness. The Bible says: "Christ also suffered for you, *leaving you an example* for you to follow in His steps" (1 Pet. 2:21, emphasis added).

Here's a question for you: When was the last time you went to Him "with loud crying and tears"? Can you remember the last time you knelt before God and opened up the wells of your broken heart to Him? If Jesus went to the Father with loud crying and tears, maybe you and I could go to Him, too. God says He will never despise a broken and contrite heart:

> God uses broken things:
> broken clouds to bring rain,
> broken grain to bring bread,
> and broken bread that brings life.

Someone once told me, "Wayne, God is still looking for men and women whose eyes are wet, whose hearts are broken and whose knees are bent—through these He will change the world." I agree.

The Sin Question

What if your *own* sin brings you to the bottom? What if you are the reason the pain is escalating?

> *Sins cannot be undone,*
> *only forgiven.*
>
> —IGOR STRAVINSKY

When you realize that your own sin has caused the downfall, remember this: Always let Jesus, not the devil, deal with your sin.

If you let the devil deal with your sin, he will riddle you with guilt and condemnation. He'll have you licking your wounds in no time. You'll throw a pity party and then follow it up with something drastic and dumb. The devil loves to deliver an anthrax-laced envelope of pain and destruction. You may have already been receiving these for years.

How do you fall into his trap where he uses your error as ammunition? Here are a few ways:

1. Leaving Sin Unresolved

It's not sin that destroys God's people; it's unresolved sin! Sin cannot be ignored, because it will cause our error to become a part of our future building. Seeds of discontent will multiply in the foundation. Unsettled accounts do not automatically clear up. Left unattended, they'll eventually rot and cause further damage.

2. **Excusing Sin**

   One of the devil's favorite tactics is to get us to justify sin, which might ease our minds for the present moment, but the consequences will not be quelled. Numbers 32:23 reminds us, "Be sure your sin will find you out." We can be certain that our sins will surface, and we will not be able to escape the consequences of its barbed intentions.

3. **Punishing Yourself**

   Another way we allow the devil to deal with our sin is to go on a guilt trip. Instead of repenting, we beat ourselves up in an effort to induce some kind of punishment to atone for our wrongdoings. We settle for a life beneath the rubble as a way to show our sorrow. This will never work. There is only one Messiah who can atone for our sins, and that is not us!

   > *It's bad when you fail morally. It's worse when you don't repent.*
   >
   > —LUIS PALAU

If we take our sin to God and let Him deal with it, the Lord says:

If we confess our sins, He is faithful and righteous to forgive us our sins and to cleanse us from all unrighteousness (1 John 1:9).

When I kept silent about my sin, my body wasted
away. . . . For day and night Your hand was heavy upon
me . . . as with the fever heat of summer. I acknowledged my sin to You, and my iniquity I did not hide;
I said, "I will confess my transgressions to the LORD";
and You forgave the guilt of my sin (Ps. 32:3-5).

God's way begins when we confess our sin openly, agreeing with
God that what we did was wrong, and then repenting. Don't run
the other way. Don't cover it. "All things are open and laid bare to
the eyes of Him with whom we have to do" (Heb. 4:13). God
knows! We might hide things from people and even fool them,
but we will never fool God. He already knows, so why not fess up?

When Adam and Eve first sinned, the only One who could
deal with and forgive their sin was the Lord. But what did they
do? Instead of going to Him, they, like Jonah, ran the other way.
God finally located the fleeing couple, and in Genesis 3:10,
a revealing sound bite unveils a problem we inherited:

[Adam] said, "I heard the sound of You in the garden,
and I was afraid . . . *so I hid myself* (emphasis added).

Don't hide. When you sin, go to God! Make sure you allow Him
to deal with your sin. Trust Him with it and cooperate with His
restoration process. There is no better way!

In you our fathers put their trust; they trusted and *you
delivered them* (Ps. 22:4, *NIV*, emphasis added).

In order for God to deliver you, you must trust Him. *Trusting
God* means that when He addresses your situation, you respond in
accordance to God's character, and not by how you *feel* about the
problem. Trust Him with your broken heart. Trust Him with your

barrenness. Trust Him with your fears, and then listen! Respond according to what God would want you to think and do, regardless of how your emotions rant and rave. Trust Him, not your feelings, and you'll be on the road to living life above the rubble!

2. Learning Life Lessons

You keep track of all my sorrows. You have collected all my tears in your bottle. You have recorded each one in your book (Ps. 56:8, *NLT*).

Please make a note of this next statement as a navigational point for your life: God never wastes a hurt.

Painful lessons can turn into precious gems. *God will never take you through a valley wherein He will not give you something of equal or greater value.* When you go through a pain or a hurt, God won't waste it. The gem will be equal to or even greater than the depth of the valley.

When someone slings mud at us, our natural tendency is to sling it back. Don't do it. If we spontaneously grab a handful of mud and sling it back, we will fail to realize that hidden in the mud are diamonds—lessons and gems intended to change our lives. We lose the gems embedded in that mud.

Even though the mud stings when it hits the flesh, be "slow to speak and slow to anger; for the anger of man does not achieve the righteousness of God" (Jas. 1:19-20). Our goal cannot be a life free of pain; instead, it must be a life that's right in God's eyes. But what do we do with the pain?

Here, I must admit, is where it gets a bit tough. In my last 30 years of ministry, I have experienced many sleepless, tear-filled nights. I have paced the floor, I have rubbed my knees raw in prayer, and I have silently wept. Give your tears all the room they need, for those tears wash away the mud to expose the diamonds.

God will never waste a hurt; Jesus can redeem any situation. In fact, He specializes in broken situations.

Not Experiencing but Learning

> Although He was a Son, He *learned obedience* from the things which He suffered (Heb. 5:8, emphasis added).

Jesus sets an example through His own life experiences. What made Him such a beautiful Savior was not that He had suffered as much as it was *the things He learned* from His sufferings.

I know many people who have suffered over the years who have let me know how much they've suffered. One man in a church in which I served as youth pastor cornered me, and with a finger pounding my chest, said, "I've been around this church afore you were born!" (He never said "before," only "afore.") "I've seen a lot of water under the bridge," he continued to lament, "survived three pastors besides the one we've got now and seen lots of wet-behind-the-ears young trainees like yourself come and go. So don't try any new stuff you learned in them Bible college classes, ya hear?"

> *The Son of God suffered unto the death, not that men might not suffer, but that their sufferings might be like His.*
>
> —GEORGE MACDONALD

He may have indeed survived some precarious years, but the lessons only seemed to harden him, not soften him. They made him crankier, not more compassionate. His suffering had stolen his once pliable heart.

Suffering *will* change you, but not necessarily for the better. You must choose your attitude.

Turning Point

There was a point in time when my whole ministry took a turn. Although I had been a Christian since 1972, it wasn't until about 12 years later that I completely relinquished my life to God. Up until this time, I treated God more as a good-luck charm than One who should be revered and served unequivocally. I can remember bargaining with God many times. I carried around an attitude that said, "I'll serve You only if and when You do what I want You to do." On the outside, I was the young pastor of a growing church; but on the inside, I was still a stubborn child.

About that time, I returned to Oregon to speak at a Youth for Christ conference. I was under a lot of stress (although I didn't realize this at the time). During the conference, I had several dizzy spells, and I could feel my heart skipping beats and erratically increasing the rate of its beat. There were times when my heart seemed to stop, and I felt a flush come over me. I actually hit my chest repeatedly as if I were doing CPR on myself! I couldn't figure out whether I was having a heart attack or just going crazy.

To change and to change for the better are two different things.

—GERMAN PROVERB

I found it to be true that when you think you are at death's door, you start evaluating your life. That's just what I did. My heart problems continued late into the night. I found myself filled with anxiety and wondering, *What's going on?* Afraid to go to sleep, I kept my desk lamp on in my hotel room, pleading with God for His healing. Finally, my eyes became as heavy as my fatigue, and I realized I would soon have to resign to the sleep I so desperately needed.

Last Will and Testament

Not knowing whether I was going to wake up the next morning, I began to write a "Last Will and Testament" letter to my wife. I finished my final words and put it on the chair next to my bed. The last thing I remember thinking was, *I'm going to sleep. If I die, then I die!*

Obviously, since you are reading this book, you know that I didn't die! Thank God! But allow me to share a portion of the letter I wrote that evening to my wife.

My dearest wife, Anna,

Tonight my heart was skipping a lot. I was starting to get dizzy spells; I have never come this close to going home before. I don't know if Jesus wants me home or not. I asked Him to let me stay, and I pleaded with Him, but I am scared. It's almost midnight and I wanted to call you, but I didn't want to bother you. If Jesus calls me home during the night, I wanted you to know how much you mean to me. I never thought I would write a letter like this. I asked Jesus and I believe He will heal me during my sleep as the Scripture says: "For He gives to His beloved even in his sleep." That is a promise that I have for tonight. However, not my will but His be done. He is Lord. I will gladly die in the service for my King. My life has been His since 1972 anyway, and He has given me many years of joy and a great family. Should Jesus take me home, please know that He will care for you, Amy and

Lord, it belongs not to my care, whether I die or live; to love and serve Thee is my share, and this Thy grace must give.

— RICHARD BAXTER

Aaron. [At that time we only had two beautiful kids.]

Do not be angry with God. He is Lord and He may do with me just as He pleases. I want to pastor the people in Hawaii and learn to be a good husband and father. There is so much I want to do and be a part of; I am torn between wanting to be with Jesus and staying here. Please forgive me for my errors and my indifference to you many times. At times I have struggled with things inside, and I don't make it a point to exalt you above my feelings and struggles. Should Jesus let me stay on I promise to do better. I must be a man of faith not only in the pulpit but also at home.

My greatest desire tonight would be that I would awake in the morning only to discard this letter and keep alive the promises to be a more godly man in my lifestyle. Tonight I am taking inventory of my life. When you brush close with death, you scan your life. I am doing that tonight. My hope is that this is what my Father wants me to do. I love you. Let the children know that their dad loves them. And should I go to be home with the Lord tonight, I will wait for you in glory until God calls you home to be with us. I am going to ask God for a mansion where both of us can stay together. Let the church know my love for them. Be Jesus to the community. Be a light.

I thank God from the bottom of my heart for having given me the privilege of being your husband.

When I woke up the next morning, I said, "Oh, yes, I am *alive!*" I reread my letter and told myself there were lessons I needed to put into practice. That evening, I reconsecrated my life to the Lord completely and unreservedly.

These life lessons resulted in huge course corrections in how I lived.

God's Amazing Grace

My grace is sufficient for you, for power is perfected in weakness (2 Cor. 12:9).

Catch what God is saying in this Scripture. When do we see God become powerful, in our strengths or in our weaknesses? Paul said, "When I am weak, then am I strong" (v. 10). God's power becomes evident when we are weak.

> *God is not disillusioned with us. He never had any illusions to begin with.*
>
> —LUIS PALAU

About three years into starting a new church plant in Hilo, I began to see things turning sour. As a young 34-year-old apprentice leader, I was making mistake after mistake, and the church began to shrink. Just when I thought I could sink no lower, one of my closest allies left abruptly and I felt completely abandoned. *What should I do?* I couldn't quit, but I didn't want to continue with things as they were either!

I have always been involved in sports, so I had it drilled into me that when you're behind, you redouble your efforts. So I did.

I started working harder, logging longer hours and increasing my drive. I stayed up longer and got less sleep, but instead of things getting better, they got increasingly worse! Finally, in desperation, I cried out to God, "God, can't You see that I am doing all this for You? You don't seem to even notice! Can't You help me just a little bit? (Don't I sound like the grumbling Israelites in the desert?) I'm doing this all alone, and I'm getting a little tired down here."

The Lord was silent.

I continued, thinking, *What is going on? God isn't helping me. I have no strength left. Has He abandoned me along with everybody else?*

I sat down on a curb and thought, *This is a terrible time. Maybe it is time to resign.* I sat silently with my head in my hands.

I guess at that moment, something of my hard shell (cast from two parts pride and one part drive) melted, leaving God sufficient opening to my heart. God then deposited a gem into my heart that I have never forgotten. He first brought back to memory the Scripture that begins with the Lord's speaking to a discouraged apostle:

> My grace is sufficient for you, for power is perfected in weakness (2 Cor. 12:9).

The apostle Paul then responds in a narrative form:

> Most gladly, therefore, I will rather boast about my weaknesses, so that the power of Christ may dwell in me (v. 9).

> Then God asked me, "Do you know why you couldn't tap in to My power? Because My power is perfected in weakness. The reason you have not seen Me strong up until now is because you've refused to be weak."

> When I heard that, my heart broke. I knew God was right. I had been stubborn. I had thought that by doubling my drive, I could make up for a loss of momentum. But in doing so, I had barred His strength. And in settling for my weakness, I found myself running on empty.

Will-power does not change men. Time does not change men. Christ does. Therefore "Let that mind be in you which was also in Christ Jesus."

—HENRY DRUMMOND

When my heart turned to His grace, my healing began. I started to see what He wanted me to do. Soon people began to sense an atmosphere of healing, and the church began to grow again—only this time in depth as well as in breadth.

3. I Love You Just Like You Are— Now *Change!*

The final thing to do when you hit rock bottom and God reveals life lessons is to change. Not know more, not realize more, not feel sorry more—*just change!*

Write down what He has said, and then record what you need to change. If you do not, you'll end up in the same rut all over again. Isn't it true that when we finally repent and He brings us out of the pit, all too often we go right back to our old ways? How quickly we forget.

> He saved them . . . and redeemed them. Then they believed His words; they sang His praise. *They quickly forgot His works* (Ps. 106:10,12-13, emphasis added).

Does that sound familiar? We cry out to God, "Oh, God, help me! God, I'll never do that again, never!" He removes the situation and what do we do? We snap back like a stretched rubber band, going right back to our old ways.

People ask me, "Wayne, why are things always going wrong in my life? It seems like God is constantly hitting me over the head with a two-by-four." I tell them, "That's probably because the only way God can get your attention is with a two-by-four! Then, when you're flat on your back, you begin to listen. But if He speaks and you return again to your old ways, He will pull His trusty two-by-four out of the closet again."

Like the old song laments, "Second verse, same as the first!"

We've got to change! When we change our ways, then He can change His methods.

"Just Die!"

After you hit bottom and your heart is broken, cry out to God and learn the life lesson He has for you, but then don't forget to change! Miss this and you will keep circling back to bedrock. The path of blessing is obedience: "If you know these things, you are blessed if you *do* them" (John 13:17, emphasis added).

Some years ago, a young man I knew tried to end his life. Someone found him just in time, rushed him to the emergency room, where the staff pumped an overdose of sleeping pills out of his stomach.

> *The only real mistake is the one from which we learn nothing.*
>
> —JOHN POWELL

I was shocked! I just couldn't believe he tried to end his own life. I was part anguished and part mad that he'd try a stupid stunt like that. I went to visit him in the hospital. When I arrived, we talked and prayed together, and slowly he recuperated. But a year later, he tried to kill himself again.

This time he took a shotgun and shot himself in the head. He missed, only blowing off one side of his head. The next time I saw him in the hospital, he had so much gauze wrapped around his head that he looked like a giant cotton swab.

I sat and reasoned with him: "Either you are a bad shot, or God is trying to tell you something. Do you think it's time to listen?"

"Well," he moaned, "I just don't want to be around."

"You really want to die and get rid of your life, don't you?" I asked.

"Yes. There's nothing left for me to live for," he replied.

I told him, "Then die."

He said, "You're not supposed to say that! You're a pastor."

"Yes, but I'm honest," I said in return, "Just die."

He hesitated and then offered, "I tried, but I missed."

"Well, next time, I will help you," I said.

"What do you mean you will help me? Do you work for Dr. Kevorkian?"

I said, "I tell you what, instead of trying so hard to get rid of your life, why don't you just give it away instead?"

"Who'd want my life?" he resigned.

"God does. And here's how you relinquish your life. Make a commitment to give Him your life and refuse to take it back. You don't want it back, anyway, do you?"

"Well, no."

"Then give it to God. It's kind of like the stuff in your house that you don't want and you give to Goodwill. Only this time, turn your life completely over, not to Goodwill, but to *God's will.*"

"And that's just like dying?" he asked.

"Better," I said. "I'll be back tomorrow and talk to you about how to give your life away."

As I left, he called after me, "I'd like to do that!"

I met with him the next day, and in the days and months that followed, he began to recuperate physically. At the same time, I watched him grow spiritually. He abandoned his life and desires and laid them all at the master's feet. Today, he's a missionary to Japan.

Steadfastness in believing doth not exclude all temptations from without. When we say a tree is firmly rooted, we do not say the wind never blows upon it.

—JOHN OWEN

Goodwill or God's Will

If you are ready for a new start, or if you are tired of the old life, then don't give it to the devil. He will have you pointing a loaded gun at your head. Instead, give whatever is left—all the broken pieces, broken dreams and shattered hopes—to God. Even if you're not at the point of taking your life, the invitation remains the same. Give your life to the only One who knows its true value!

Each of us has rock-bottom experiences, but it is in the midst of the bile that some of life's greatest lessons will be discov-

God will not look you over for medals, degrees, and diplomas but for scars.

—ELBERT HUBBARD

ered. They may come as a result of a storm, or they may come as a result of an unanticipated collapse. When you are at the bottom, don't give up, don't justify yourself, and don't blame others for your lot in life. Turn your life over to God's will.

When you're in a whale's belly splashing in bile, cry out to God. He's listening and waiting on the beach that leads to Nineveh. And when you have been deposited on the seashore, don't look for a ticket office to Tarshish. Instead, listen for a familiar voice inviting you to a new beginning: "Come, follow Me."

WHY DOES GOD LET US STRUGGLE?

Why does God let us struggle? This is a common question and one that many people ask, especially in difficult times. I have often wondered that myself.

Rephrase the question and you'll hear a similar question: If God is such a loving God, why does He allow bad things to happen?

Let's begin by asking someone who understood struggles. He was persecuted and tested. He failed miserably and had to wrestle his way back through personal doubts and fears. Let's ask him. His name is Peter.

Beloved, do not be surprised at the fiery ordeal among you, which comes upon you for your testing, as though some strange thing were happening to you (1 Pet. 4:12).

We grow because we struggle, we learn and overcome.

—R. C. ALLEN

Let's settle one thing right up front—we all hit speed bumps; we all experience setbacks. Don't consider it strange. It's not abnormal. It's something all of us experience. Struggles will be inevitable in our lives. Whether they are financial hardships, health problems or disintegrated relationships, we will struggle—guaranteed.

However, it's not the struggle that sets you back. I have experienced many struggles myself and have counseled hundreds through devastating events and seasons of pain. Some come through better and others come through bitter. What's the difference?

It's not the struggle that determines your success or failure. It's what you do *during* the struggle. While God cares about what you are going through, He is infinitely more concerned with what you are allowing to go through you!

There Is Good in the Struggle

Isn't there some kind of pill we can take to help us bypass all the effort? We would like to have our struggles removed. But be careful what you wish and pray for. You just might get it!

If you eliminate struggle, you also eliminate much of what brings character and depth to your life. According to scientists, a hatching baby chick *must* peck its own way out of the eggshell. If someone took the shell and cracked it open for the baby chick, it would die. The circulatory system of the chick is activated and developed in its struggle to break free from the shell. If the struggle is removed, so is the baby chick's ability to develop and, consequently, live.

One of the best classrooms in the world for developing character is struggle. It provides lessons that bring depth to our lives. Without struggle, we would lack the God-designed program that builds our character muscles. We *must* be willing to experience struggle for the sake of growth.

It's not the struggle, but what you do within the struggle that makes all the difference.

"But, Wayne, that's crazy!" is the response I usually get. "Why in the world would I ever be willing to experience struggle?"

I think the answer to this question is articulated eloquently at a Vietnam veterans rehabilitation center where, on a brass plaque, these words are etched:

I asked God for strength that I might achieve greatness,
> But I was made weak that I might learn humbly to obey.

I asked for health that I might do many things,
> But I was given infirmity that I might do better things.

I asked for riches that I might be happy,
> But I was given poverty that I might become wise.

I asked for power that I might lead men,
> But I was given humility that I might need only God.

I asked for all things so that I could enjoy life,
> But God gave me life that I might learn to enjoy all things.

I got nothing that I asked for,
But everything that I had hoped for.
Despite myself, all of my deepest prayers were
answered,
And now I among all men am most richly blessed.

Isn't that beautiful? Its author learned a life principle: We must be willing to struggle for the sake of growth. There is no other way.

God Is for Us

If the foundations are destroyed, what can the righteous do? (Ps. 11:3).

The first item of priority we need to establish is to set our compasses correctly. If our foundational perspectives are inaccurate, then every conclusion we arrive at will also be inaccurate.

One of the best classrooms in the world for developing character is struggle.

I play golf. Not well, mind you, but I play. I don't know too much about the game, but I do know this: If at the point of contact I hit the ball just half an inch off from where it should have been hit, it will be miles off course. However, if the club strikes the ball precisely where it is supposed to be hit, and the follow-through is accurate, then the trajectory will be predictable as the ball lands softly in the middle of the fairway some 300 yards ahead. (That's about my distance. You know, Tiger's and mine.)

With this in mind, here's one of the first items of business in understanding the plaguing question about struggle: God always works for our good!

If God is for us, who can be against us? (Rom. 8:31, *NIV*).

We need to be clear that *God is for us* before proceeding on this topic. He will not allow suffering to touch us unless it has first passed across His desk and He has approved it. First Peter 2:9 tells us that we "are a chosen race, a royal priesthood, a holy nation, *a people for God's own possession*" (emphasis added).

This is an interesting phrase in the original Greek. The *King James Version* translates it: "a peculiar people." This is a unique way to describe the people of God. (Although I do know a few I would describe in those terms!)

> *Good timber does not grow with ease. The stronger the wind, the stronger the trees.*
>
> —J. WILLARD MARRIOTT

In the original language, "peculiar" is translated with the terms "in" and "around." It is saying: We are God's possessions, and He has us "in His embrace" and His protection "surrounds us." Therefore, if anything touches our lives, it has first passed through His encircling care before it reaches us. And if it does, then God has permitted it because He knows that He can use it for our own good.

God knows what we can handle, so if He has allowed something in our lives, we can be assured that God has already authorized it for our lives, as painful as it may seem:

God is faithful, who will not allow you to be tempted beyond what you are able (1 Cor. 10:13).

God's Love Includes Struggle

Everything God does in our lives is based upon His character, and God's character is love. His goal is to disciple us, and discipleship always includes its companion, discipline:

For those whom the Lord loves He disciplines (Heb. 12:6).

God's discipline comes out of His love. God births everything into our lives because He loves us. When we talk about

The alternative to discipline is disaster.

—VANCE HAVNER

struggles, we must always define them in light of God's changeless character and not by our limited experience.

Explaining God's Love

A person recently wrote me a letter saying, "I don't understand your God. I came to your church and you took a stance against homosexuality. You said to 'draw lines and build bridges,' mean-ing we should reach out to the sinner but be clear about sin. I think God is partial and discriminatory against certain groups of people. I just can't agree with your God!"

The stance God takes against sin is not because He hates peo-ple. He doesn't discipline us because of hate. Rather, it's because of love. Although we may not always understand His stance, we must always remember to interpret it through the character of a loving God. *Everything that touches our lives—including struggle and discipline—is wrapped in His love.*

Thousands of cars are stolen in the state of California each year, but in 1984, one auto theft made front-page news. Nearly every radio and television station covered the incident. Why all the fuss?

As the story goes, a man who owned a summer cabin was hav-ing some rodent problems. In order to control the mice, he pre-pared some crackers laced with poison to use for bait. He got in his car to leave his summer cabin, but forgetting his glasses in the house, he darted back in to retrieve them. While he was in the house, a thief jumped into his idling car and sped off.

When the owner realized the theft and remembered that he had left the crackers on the front seat, he quickly called the police. Law-enforcement officials issued an all-points bulletin alerting the thief to return the car immediately. They began a desperate search to find the unaware burglar. Television stations donated prime-time spots and radio stations filled the airwaves in attempts to find the driver.

Why do you think they were trying so desperately to locate the thief? Was it in order to punish him? It was to save his life!

So it is with the heart of our Savior. He desperately pursues us not because He hates us. He disciplines us not out of sadistic motives. *He pursues us because He wants to save our lives!* Regardless of how it looks, rest assured, God will always work for our good.

Trust Him. He's after you to save your life!

Trials are medicines which our gracious and wise Physician prescribes because we need them; and he proportions the frequency and weight of them to what the case requires. Let us trust his skill and thank him for his prescription.

—SIR ISACC NEWTON

Suffering Deepens Credibility

During his Bible-college years, my son, Aaron, and I often shared our devotional times together at a local coffee shop. One day we discussed what it takes to be a good leader. We discussed and agreed on several nonnegotiables, such as character, faith, people skills, vision, knowledge and the ability to communicate.

Aaron, who was 21 years old at the time, said with a wry smile, "Then I think I'll be ready soon, Dad!"

"Not yet. There's still one thing you lack," I replied.

"What's that, Dad?" he asked.

"You haven't yet suffered enough."

We find this to be true in the life of Paul. He was a well-trained Pharisee who had studied under the renowned Gamaliel. Paul exhibited all the knowledge, contacts and gifts of a leader. However, when God qualified him for ministry, Paul had some prerequisites to meet. Paul was sent to the house of Ananias, who was commanded by the Lord to pray for him (see Acts 9). Somewhat reticent with this divine assignment, Ananias balked at the request. He knew of Paul's qualifications for leadership, but he also knew of Paul's deadly disdain for Christians:

> But Ananias answered, "Lord, I have heard from many about this man, how much harm he did to Your saints at Jerusalem; and here he has authority from the chief priests to bind all who call on Your name" (vv. 13-14).

Then the Lord revealed to Ananias (as He does to each of us) one of the purposes of suffering:

> He is a chosen instrument of Mine, to bear My name before the Gentiles and kings and the sons of Israel; for I will show him *how much he must suffer for My name's sake* (vv. 15-16, emphasis added).

Paul had been chosen, but he wasn't yet complete. Suffering readies us for His purposes and His assignment. Don't fear the times of lack. Make do with what you have. Don't fear seasons of dryness. Dig deep. Don't fear times when you feel unfairly treated. Stand secure.

Growing Deep Through Suffering

Mr. A. Bailey was an apple farmer, one of the best. During a season of prolonged drought, all the orchards in the valley dried up for lack of moisture. The apple crop seemed destined to doom. Mr. Bailey was called in and asked why his orchard was so green while everyone else's was so dry.

He replied, "My trees can go another two weeks without a drop of water."

"Well, how'd you do that?" the other curious farmers prodded.

"When my trees were young, I frequently withheld water from them. Because of that, they had to send their roots deeper into the soil to find water. Now, while other trees are dying, mine are drinking moisture at a much greater depth."

When others curse the seasons of suffering, be sure that

Suffering readies us for His purposes and His assignment. Don't fear the times of lack. Make do with what you have. Don't fear seasons of dryness. Dig deep. Don't fear times when you feel unfairly treated. Stand secure.

you invest your energy by sending your roots deeper in order to draw water from a greater depth.

Suffering Defeats Cynicism

> [He is] the One who so wonderfully comforts and strengthens us in our hardships. . . . So that we can pass on . . . this same help and comfort God has given us (2 Cor. 1:3-4, *TLB*).

I have studied under many professors in classes and seminars at Bible college in my lifetime. Many of them were astute, outstanding in their academic pursuits. They impressed me with their intellectual feats. Yet the ones who influenced me most were not those who taught solely from academic achievement or scholarly books. The ones who influenced me most were those who taught me out of their scars.

These men and women walked their faith and experienced the very lessons they taught. They had survived difficult situations and adverse circumstances; and when they shared their experiences, there was a ring of credibility to everything they said.

Adoniram Judson was one of the famed missionaries to Burma, also known as Myanmar. God used him to bring great revival—thousands upon thousands came to know the Lord. When he first arrived in Burma, however, he had to endure a great deal of struggle. People actually hated him and fought against his ministry attempts. On top of all of that, several of his own children died due to accidents, fever or sickness.

In the first seven years, he saw only one convert to Christ. In the following 17 months, he was imprisoned—shackled and hung in chains, which gnawed into his flesh and left him badly scarred for life. When he was finally released, he immediately went to the overseer of a section in Burma to gain permission to preach the gospel. The ruler said, "No, I cannot allow you to enter."

Your scars bear the loudest testimony you may ever preach.

"Why not?" asked Judson.

The ruler replied, "We are not so foolish as to be taken in by the words you say, so I am not worried by what you will speak. However, I am troubled that the people may be convinced by the scars that you bear."

Words are cheap, but scars run deep.

God works through each and every scar and will never waste a hurt. He uses scars in your life to impact another life that is hurting and struggling. *Your scars bear the loudest testimony you may ever preach.*

Struggles and Tests Increase Our Faith

Consider it all joy, my brethren, when you encounter various trials, knowing that the *testing of your faith* produces endurance. And let endurance have its perfect result, so that you may be perfect and complete, lacking in nothing (Jas. 1:2-4, emphasis added).

The testing of my faith produces endurance. In other words, it develops character. If my faith remains untested, it may produce a moral philosophy, but it will not generate a fruitful faith. When God tests my faith, *He activates it.* Only then can I be enrolled in His program to make me "perfect and complete, lacking in nothing."

My favorite area of learning is linguistics. I love languages. I've studied Spanish, Latin, Japanese and Hebrew. My most challenging subject, however, was Greek. We started with 36 wide-eyed students in the fall, and by graduation, we had been reduced to 6. I always kept excellent grades and remained challenged till the end. Here's why.

Every morning we went to Greek class, and we always could expect a test. At precisely 8 A.M., the bell would ring and the professor would say, "Please take out a fresh piece of paper and a pencil. We are going to have a test." Then he would write some vocabulary words on the board, and we would have to translate them. Other times, he'd chalk a verb or two, and we'd be given five minutes to parse them. I knew that each morning, without fail, we would have a test, and because of that, I stayed on top of my homework. I attained straight As in the class, because I knew that we would have daily tests and I prepare for them.

Tests help you to be productive. Without them, you will not produce, because you are not being held accountable. God tests your faith for that very reason. *He knows that faith will not produce fruit without being tested.*

Testing or Tempting

Let me give you an easy Greek lesson. There is a big difference between *testing* and *tempting.* The Greek word "to test" is the word *dokimon,* which means "to locate a weakness with the purpose of strengthening and reinforcing it." The word "to tempt" in the Greek is the word *periazo,* which means "to find a weakness with the goal of using that weakness to destroy the person."

The devil is a tempter who is on the lookout for our weaknesses. When the devil locates them, he can *tempt* us. His goal is to find a weak spot and capitalize on it in order to defeat us. In fact, his intention will always be to steal, kill and destroy (see John 10:10).

God, on the other hand, *tests* us to make sure we are strong enough. God will never *tempt* us because His character is love. God, like a finish carpenter who has just built a custom bookshelf, has purposed the completed project to succeed and last. He will examine and evaluate its readiness by putting weight or pressure on it. This check will reveal any weakness or fragility. Should He find it flawed, He will reinforce it in order to sustain the weight it is designed to hold.

God does the same with you. When He puts pressure on you and it reveals a weakness, don't give up. Don't drop out. He is about to reinforce and strengthen an area of your life so that you will be able to sustain the weight of His assignment and commission. *It is through testing that God makes us ready!*

Desire Versus Readiness

Just because you have a desire for marriage does not always mean

that you are ready for it. Your desire to be prosperous does not always mean you are ready for financial prosperity. God will put you through tests to reveal any area that needs reinforcing— your attitude, integrity, character, competency, compassion, stewardship and more! So let the tests begin. Why? Because He wants you to succeed.

Desire seldom equals readiness.

One of my all-time favorite instructors was my sixth-grade math teacher, Mr. Hayes. I was his class pet. I am not sure why, especially when math was not my strongest subject. Maybe he felt sorry for me. Whatever the case, he always gave me extra help and personal attention.

I remember one final exam in particular. After he had passed out the tests, I took one look at the problems and groaned. I was lost before I had even started. Mr. Hayes walked up and down the aisles between our desks. As he drew up near mine, he came to a stand still. He noticed that 15 minutes had slid by, and I hadn't made a mark on my paper yet. I kept staring at a blank answer sheet as he cleared his throat, "Ahem!"

"I think I have a hemorrhage in my brain, Mr. Hayes," I whined. "Do you think I could be excused from this test?"

"Only if you fall down right now and die," he quipped. I was unprepared for his witty touché. Then as if changing gears, he slowly began to speak to me in monotones. Pointing to the first problem, he said, "Wayne, do you remember what 8 multiplied by 7 is?"

"Sixty-four," I replied confidently. (You can see why I was in a remedial math class in the sixth grade.)

"Ooh!" he moaned, as if he had just gotten a cramp in his leg. I tried again, "Fifty-six?"

"Mm hmm! Okay, write that down right here," he said, pointing to the part of an equation where I had erred. His interrogation continued: "What does x equal?"

"I don't know," I said sheepishly. I felt bad. I couldn't figure out what a letter of the alphabet was doing in a forest of numbers.

"Look on the board. What is the given for x?"

"Oh, I see. It says that x equals 20!"

"Mm hmm! Alright, now what is 2 multiplied by x?"

"Oh! Um, 40?" (Actually, I guessed.)

"Good guess!" He had read my mind, but now I was off to the races! Mr. Hayes stood there until I finally completed the entire test.

As I think back on that memory, I still have to chuckle. Mr. Hayes never gave me any answers, but he tested me with questions again and again until I got it. He wasn't testing me in order to get me to fail. No! His testing was designed to guarantee my success.

When you understand God's heart, you will see your struggles in a very different light.

God is committed to you and your future. Because of that, He understands that your faith must be tested before He can build on it. He allows tests in your life not because He dislikes you but because He is committed to your success. He will never leave your side. While He won't do the work for you, He will stay with you till the end.

When you understand God's heart, you will see your struggles in a very different light. Instead of working against God, you will cooperate. You won't be looking for a way out with a trumped-up hemorrhage; and in the end, you'll hear His words: "Well done, good and faithful servant" (Matt. 25:21, *NIV*).

Struggles Prompt Us to Change

Sometimes it takes a painful situation to make us change our ways (see Prov. 20:30).

People usually resist change until the pain of remaining the same is greater than the effort it takes to change. One of God's most effective tools to increase our motivation beyond good intentions is *pain*. The truth is, *If we never struggle, we will probably never change.* Too many times, when we're in a bad relationship or situation, we wait until it gets infected before we cry out, "Lord, I can't stand it anymore!"

Then God says, "Change."

"Okay, I will."

"That's just what I wanted you to do in the first place."

Prayer Time or Complaining Session

There are times when my prayers turn into complaining sessions. Occasionally, my wife and I get into an argument. When we get into these occasional differences of opinion, I go to my knees, only to start confessing all of my wife's sins: "Oh, God! I can't believe this woman that You gave me. Do You realize how many faults she came with when You gave her to me? You've got to change her, Lord! Amen."

One of God's most effective tools to increase our motivation beyond good intentions is pain. If we never struggle, we will probably never change.

Now that I've "prayed it through" (I try to practice what I preach), I get up from my knees. However, I've done more complaining than praying, so my wife and I are back in the same argument again in no time.

The next time I pray, I wrestle more than usual because of the realization that I've been in this predicament before. My conscience begins to burn and the fatigue begins to break my heart.

My prayers now carry fewer complaints and more groans of intercession, which allow God's refining process to begin.

My desperation cracks an opening in my stubbornness, and I start to hear the faint voice of God:

> When was the last time you took a few moments to explain things to her? Have you walked with her through her difficult roadblocks and struggles? Are you so proud that you cannot take the time to hear her concerns and defer to her level of understanding?

Sometimes God gets a little too personal:

> When was the last time you helped her clean the house? I mean purposefully stayed home and did some house-work with her.

I think hard and answer, "Back in '73."

This time I return from my prayer closet changed. Without the pain, I'd still be blaming my wife today! It has taken a painful situation to get me to see myself clearly enough to demand change.

Making Course Corrections

> And they were being baptized by him in the Jordan River, as they confessed their sins. "Therefore *bear fruit in keeping with repentance*" [said John the Baptist] (Matt. 3:6,8, emphasis added).

Until we begin to change, every church activity—weekly atten-dance, prayer, tithing and worship—is reduced to religious froth. We have designed a religion that knows everything there is to know about love, but we can't love. We know everything there is to know about forgiveness, but we can't forgive. We sing songs about joy, but we're usually depressed!

One of the major reasons for stress is that we live incongruent lives. We believe one thing but live another. We know what we should do, but our lives are inconsistent with our knowledge. We see the warning lights, but we ignore them and even complain about them.

It's like the oil light on the dashboard of our car. When it lights up, we have several options. We can check it out, complain that the red light is distracting or crawl under the dash and yank out the wires. Or, if you're anything like me, you can blame your wife.

> *We can either sit and decide "who's wrong" or join forces and attack "what's wrong" instead.*

"Honey, how long has this red light been on in the car?"

"I guess about two weeks," she replied.

"Two whole weeks! Do you know *why* that light is on?"

"I thought if it was really important the light would get brighter and start making a sound, like a buzz or a beep or something."

"Honey, this is a car, not a game show!" I retorted.

God gives us warning lights when we are struggling. We can either get upset with each other or we can change and make the necessary corrections. We can either sit and decide "who's wrong" or join forces and attack "what's wrong" instead.

Keep Listening

My daughter, Amy, had the most obnoxious alarm clock in the world. It sort of sounded as if someone were trying to clear his or her throat but not quite able to do so. It was the most aggravating noise. This device would go off in the morning making a racket that would raise the dead, but still Amy would lie there fast asleep.

After 20 minutes, I would stomp to her bedroom and attempt to rouse her. Still, I could sense no detectable motion. Along with the demonic contraption blaring at enough force to register on the local Richter scale, I'd yell, "Amy, the whole household and neighborhood are now awake. Would you like to join us?"

Don't ever let God's warnings become commonplace. God's involvement in your life is a precious thing.

You can become oblivious to alarms if they become common. Start pushing the snooze button, and after a while, you'll do it in your sleep.

Don't ever let God's warnings become commonplace. It's a habit that must be avoided at all costs. God's involvement in your life is a precious thing. At times you may find yourself wanting God to just leave you alone, but don't let that tendency take root in you. That bent will become a propensity, which will develop into a predisposition. This then takes on a life of its own, and you will find that same tendency in your marriage, your devotion to God and your commitments to people.

Someone once told me, "When the precious becomes common, it is soon replaced."

Don't let what God says to you ever become commonplace. Never let His gifts, your family or your spouse slip into dull ordinariness. Keep His voice vibrant and your heart ever attentive.

Struggles Develop Proven Character

The best character classroom in the world is struggle. God understands this so well that He even allowed His own Son, Jesus, to struggle:

Although He was a Son, He learned obedience from the
things which He suffered (Heb. 5:8).

Jesus learned obedience from the things He suffered. What makes
you valuable isn't that you've suffered. What makes you valuable
is what you've *learned* through your suffering. Jesus learned obedience. The question for you and me remains: What have we
learned from our suffering?

I am convinced that life consists of 10 percent what happens
to you and 90 percent what you learn from what happens to you.
You choose what you learn. One of the most beautiful classrooms
for learning character is in the red-hot cauldron of struggle.

As you allow God to work within you, you need to "keep on
rejoicing" (1 Pet. 4:13). When God is standing over your shoul-
der and testing you, keep on rejoicing. You know that it is coming from the heart of a loving Father. Rejoice! Don't let the devil
steal your joy in the midst of your struggles. We see this again in
the book of James: "Consider it all joy . . . when you encounter
various trials" (1:2).

God Is the Master Potter

Some time ago, there was a potter who was a master among pot-
ters. He had the seemingly supernatural ability to create beautiful, translucent vessels out of humble, opaque clay. He baked the
vases in an old-fashioned kiln. He used no timer except his intu-
ition and years of experience to determine their readiness.
A moment too long and the vessels would overbake, causing
hairline cracks to form in the glaze as it cooled. Remove them
prematurely, and the vessels would retain an excessive amount
of moisture, rendering them useless.

One day, an admirer came to ask about the beautiful mas-
terpieces. He inquired, "Sir, how in the world do you know when

to take the vessels out of the oven? You have neither a thermometer nor a timer. How could you possibly know the moment when they are finished to perfection?"

The potter answered, "I do it the old way."

The curious onlooker continued his inquiry: "And how is that, may I ask?"

The master carefully explained, "I take the vessels, put them in the oven, close the door and let them bake. At a certain time, I pull one of the vessels from the oven and test it with a sharp flick on its rim. If it responds only with a thud, then I know there is still water in that vessel. I put it back in the oven and close the door. Later, I remove it and thump it again. If there is still a thud, I return it to the oven. After more time, I take the vessel and give it a gentle but sharp strike on its rim. If this time it sings, then I know it is ready to be removed."

God is the master potter. He wants you to become your very best, so He has to put you through the hot kilns of life's struggles. He slides you inside the oven and closes the door.

Somewhere in the furnace—just as He did with Shadrach, Meshach and Abednego—the Lord walks in. No, He doesn't give us all the answers, but He does walk us all the way through. In the process, something changes inside of us. We understand Him; we trust Him more. And like Paul and Silas in their prison-cell kiln, at just about midnight, we start to sing!

The master potter has great plans for you. Cooperate with Him and watch what He can do in your life. Why does God let you struggle? Because it's the fastest way to become a fine and finished masterpiece!

CHAPTER 3

HOW TO MAKE LIFE SIMPLE AGAIN

Do you ever yearn for the simpler days? I do.

I remember growing up in lush, rain-graced Palolo Valley on the Hawaiian island of Oahu. During my youth, my favorite day of the week was Saturday. That's when my brother, Gary, and I would jump on our bicycles and ride into town.

We would ride all the way to Waikiki Beach, park our bikes, run out on the pier and practice our cannonballs and jackknifes into the clear blue waves. Then we would climb up onto the slippery, moss-covered breakwall and jump from point to point, splashing around whenever we happened to fall in.

In the early afternoon, we would get back onto our bikes and go to the matinee. We would eat popcorn—not just plain, white popcorn but colored popcorn. What a treat! Sometimes we watched 3-D movies and wore those geeky glasses with one red lens and one blue lens. Since it was dark and no one could recognize us, we'd scream like girls.

After the matinee, we'd saddle up on our bikes and ride to an old deli for a hot bowl of Japanese noodles known to locals as *saimin*. We'd sit around a horseshoe-shaped counter, spinning our stools and slurping our noodles in sauce turned black by soy sauce and pepper. We'd have fun bantering with the old Japanese man who served us. He could only speak Japanese, and we'd make believe we agreed with whatever he was saying. He'd go on for an hour or so before we could make our getaway to the Palolo stream.

The stream, fed by the Koolau mountain range, would be laden with guppies. We'd fashion homemade spears out of discarded coat hangers and spear crayfish and, if we were lucky, a rubber slipper or two. Often, we would lie there in the foliage smelling the wild ginger and pungent guava fruit ripening.

Then, at about four o'clock in the afternoon, we'd make our way up to Red Hill where we played marbles—for keeps! Our goal was to go home with pockets bulging full of prize marbles. My brother and I would spill out the contents of our pockets onto the bed and count our take. The one who had the most would gain bragging rights until the next Saturday's contest at Red Hill.

Every Saturday we had the same fun all over again. We'd laugh our way home at the end of the day. Savoring these memories has sustained me for years now. Oh, the simple days, the innocent memories of yesteryear!

For some, the simple days are nostalgic. They may make you sing, "Oh, the good life!" For others, the simpler days are an escape. I remember when the Beatles came out with the song,

"Yesterday, all my troubles seemed so far away. Now it seems like the kids are here to stay."

Isn't that how it went? I can't quite remember.

Crowded, Empty Lives

How do we restore simplicity to a life that has gotten so complicated? Let's look to a prophet named Isaiah. He talked about what happens when our lives get too complicated:

> Woe to those who add house to house and join field to field, until there is no more room, so that you have to live alone in the midst of the land! (Isa. 5:8).

In other words, woe to those who add so much to their lives that there is no more room. Their plates are too full and their lives have become too complex. The unfortunate consequence is "You have to live alone in the midst of the land." *Your life is full of activity, but those activities no longer breathe life,* and the chest cavity that used to contain a warm, beating heart is now cold and hollow.

Isaiah wrote these words in the year 600 B.C., over 2,700 years ago. Yet he seemed to understand our twenty-first century with crystal clarity.

In the very next verses, Isaiah continued:

> In my ears the LORD of hosts has sworn, "Surely, many houses shall become desolate, even great and fine ones, without occupants. For ten acres of vineyard will yield only one bath [a little bit] of wine" (vv. 9-10).

He explained that 10 acres of energy expended will produce very little. All the busyness of our activities will produce hardly any fruit at all. Woe to us indeed!

"Ah, look at all the lonely people," sang the Beatles in the '60s. The message of that song, "Eleanor Rigby," is still alive and well today as we continue to live complex and lonely lives.

Joy is prayer—Joy is strength—Joy is a net of love by which you can catch souls.

— MOTHER TERESA

In a children's book, titled *The All Better Book*, the preadolescent authors pose some fairly philosophical questions. Answers to one question asked of eight-year-olds and nine-year-olds intrigued me. Here's the question:

With billions of people in the world, someone should figure out a system where no one is lonely. What do you suggest?

Here are the answers:

People should find lonely people and ask them their names and addresses. Then find people who aren't lonely and ask them their names and addresses. When you have an even number of each, assign the lonely people to match up with the not lonely people. Publish their names in the newspaper so that they can get together.

—Kalani, age eight

Make foods that talk to you. For instance, when you poke your fork into some food it could say, "How are you doing?" When you cut into a hamburger it could say, "What did you do today?"

—Max, age nine

If someone doesn't feel like they are pretty, you could say, "Hey, you are!" Or you could say, "At least you're a lot prettier than someone I know that has really big, bulgy eyes."

—Kathy, age eight

Sing a song to yourself, stomp your feet or read a book. Because sometimes when I think that no one loves me, I do one of those things.

—Brian, age eight

We live in a world filled with Brians—lonely people left only to sing songs to themselves, stomp their feet or rent a video every night to amuse themselves. They watch endless streams of talk shows just to hear someone talk. They enter into destructive relationships, thinking that *any* companionship is better than none at all. Or they pour themselves into their jobs, working long hours and holidays and weekends. Some even read a book, just like this one, all alone.

Grief can take care of itself, but to get the full value of joy you must have somebody to divide it with.

—MARK TWAIN

With billions of people in the world, someone ought to figure out a way to make the lonely feel welcomed and loved. Someone has figured it out. His name is God. He has filled a Book full of ways we can make our lives simple again. He can guide us with the best guidance system known to man, and He will warn us when life is being crowded out and lonesomeness is setting in.

God's Early Warning Systems

A few years ago, I was in Sapporo (a city in northern Japan) sleeping soundly at a friend's house. Suddenly, in the middle of the night, the whole house started to shake. I got up and hung on to the windowsill. The ground beneath me was rolling like waves of liquid earth. After 20 seconds or so, it settled down and we went back to sleep. Little did we realize the devastating effect that earthquake had on the little island Okushiri, just off the shore of Hokkaido.

Because of this killer earthquake (it rocked the Richter scale at 7.8), a devastating tidal wave had been immediately unleashed on a sleepy little fishing village at the base of Okushiri. Hundreds of people were killed without warning. It was devastating!

Today, because of such sudden tragedies as the one at Okushiri, early warning detectors are being placed everywhere. Some are designed for twisters, which can spring up in a matter of seconds and have the potential to lay waste to anything or anyone in their path. Other early warning detectors can pick up seismic activity, which indicates a volcanic eruption on the big island of Hawaii. And still others can warn of an oncoming earthquake and any resulting killer tidal wave.

In Hawaii, on the first day of every month, a siren sounds at precisely 11:45 A.M. A message on every radio station follows: "This is a test of the civil defense early warning system." Hawaii relies heavily on this early warning system as its tiny islands are prone to hurricanes, tidal waves and even aerial military attacks like that of Pearl Harbor. This monthly test keeps Hawaii well prepared.

God has some early warning systems for our lives as well. They are not as obvious as bright yellow sirens or blaring radio broadcasts, but they are every bit as noticeable if we pay close attention.

1. When Close Relationships Begin to Suffer

A red alert, five-engine alarm should ring any time we sacrifice loved ones for work or a busy schedule. This can happen when we get busy trying to make a name for ourselves, make money or make the climb up the corporate ladder. I'll say this just once—please don't miss its magnitude—no amount of success in the marketplace will ever make up for failure at home.

Someone once explained it this way: "The darkest place of a lighthouse is at its own base." This can sometimes be true of even the best families. We can be well known in the marketplace, our community or our neighborhood, but it is dark at home. We take our dearest ones for granted, skipping over those who matter most, and they suffer. At first they suffer silently, and we *almost* notice, but we're too busy. Then the suffering gets not so silent—verbal assaults flare into family feuds and relationships become "irreconcilable differences."

One early warning signal of a complicated life is when close relationships flicker and the home fires die out. Granted, we live in a society that's on fast-forward, a dog-eat-dog world. And we live on a street where everyone is keeping up with the Joneses. Yet echoing in our hearts is heaven's siren:

> Don't let the world around you squeeze you into its own mould, but let God re-make you so that your whole attitude of mind is changed. Thus you will prove in practice that the will of God is good, acceptable to him and perfect (Rom. 12:2, *Phillips*).

God is showing us an early warning signal. This signal may not be as jolting as an attention-getting attack siren, but it should be. It should be every bit as jarring and equally terrifying. If we can detect the early warning signals, then we can avoid a lot of devastation and loneliness.

Daddy's home. Some time ago, I was writing a lot of songs and Maranatha Music bought some and recorded them. Of course, before I go any further, I should warn you not to look for them on any best-selling CD, soundtrack or worship album.

They weren't that hot, but at least someone bought them. Well, executives at Maranatha called me after purchasing a number of them and they said they were interested in my coming on board with them. In fact, they wanted to sponsor me to do some recording.

They said, "We will pay for the recording of a set of songs. And we also want to contract you to become a spokesperson for Maranatha. You'll be traveling around the country to help us promote Christian music."

A red alert, five-engine alarm should go off any time we sacrifice loved ones for work or a busy schedule.

"Wow!" was all I could say. Inside I was thinking, *That's my dream! It's what I've always wanted to do. Here's my big chance!*

Then they added, "You will have to travel more than 200 days out of the year, because you have to be able to sell the music and market it."

I was excited, but I asked them if I could pray about it and get back to them. I went home and talked to my wife, Anna, about this opportunity. Her face dropped. She sighed and said, "Oh, but you're already traveling so much."

"Yeah, but I can do this!" I said quickly. "Anyway," further trying to convince her, "it could really financially benefit our family."

At that time, we were a young family—our daughter, Amy, was four years old and our son, Aaron, was just two—and we were barely making ends meet. Being the epitome of graciousness, my wife simply said, "Well, I'll support whatever you feel God is telling you to do." And we left it at that. In my heart though, I was really excited.

A few days later, I was darting out to the airport for another speaking engagement, and I passed by my daughter's room.

Anna was sitting with her on the bed laughing and telling her a story. I stopped to say good-bye. Just then, I noticed a big picture of me propped up on Amy's dresser. It was an 8-by-10 inch portrait of me in the middle of her little room.

I was honored and said, "Wow, Honey, what's this?" I held it up, "How do I deserve the honor of having this flattering portrait of me placed on Amy's dresser?"

Without any contention at all, Anna quietly said, "I didn't want my daughter to ever forget who her daddy is."

I immediately made the necessary corrections, pruned a few commitments and basically died to that "dream." I soon realized, though, that it was a lesser dream. God had a much greater dream in store for me. His plan allowed me the time to be with my family and friends, and to enjoy the wonderful experiences He had planned. I gave up a lesser dream for a greater dream.

It is important to become aware that at every moment of our life we have an opportunity to choose joy. . . . It is in the choice that our true freedom lies, and that freedom is, in the final analysis, the freedom to love.

—HENRI J. M. NOUWEN

Thankfully, God had me marry a subtle wife whom He used as an early warning signal long before I lost my family.

Barbara Bush, in speaking at the commencement exercises of Wellesley College, said something I've never forgotten: "The health of this great country will not be primarily determined by what happens in the White House, but rather by what happens at *your* house."[1]

I agree!

2. When There Is a Diminished Joy

The joy of the LORD is your strength (Neh. 8:10).

Joy is like a barometer in our lives indicating how strong we are in any situation. It's the measure of how healthy we are on the *inside*. If there's no joy, then the Bible says we are weak. If there is joy, then there is strength. Always watch for your level of joy. Is your reservoir full or is it empty?

A joyless life can strike you at the most unexpected moments. Layers of silent compromise will one day startle you like the discovery of an advanced cancer. You were feeling ill for a while, but never thought anything about it. One day you realize that the joy that once caused even the simplest activities in your marriage to sparkle has lost its luster. It can happen in your role as a father or a mother, as a student or an employee. In fact, it can happen in any role you play. Perhaps the joy of attending church services or volunteering for ministries no longer holds the excitement it once did. *Essentially, you're fulfilling a role, but it's not fulfilling anymore.*

All of these areas begin to add up—joyless relationships, joyless work, joyless living—and life becomes complicated. You start fighting, locking horns and driving home with a discontented heart, and it all comes down to one simple thing: *The joy is gone!*

The devil's target is your joy. Did you know that *your joy is a primary target* of the adversary of our souls? But the devil can't steal your salvation. If Jesus Christ is your Lord and Savior, then your salvation is not based on your performance or effort; instead, it is founded and protected on the effort of the sinless One at Calvary. It's wrapped up in His blood, not yours. I'm so glad for that!

Thus, the enemy opts for his second choice. Since he cannot steal your salvation, he tries to steal the *joy* of your salvation. He knows that if he can steal your joy, then your soul will begin to wither even in the most favorable conditions. You'll remain a Christian, but you'll be a joyless, weak one. You'll remain converted, but you're no longer contagious. Redemption may have flowed *to* you, but it will not flow *through* you.

Restore to me the joy of Your salvation and sustain me with a willing spirit (Ps. 51:12).

The devil will try to steal your joy so that you will defeat yourself. You see, the devil cannot steal your marriage. He has no authority to do that. Instead, he steals the joy of your marriage and then hopes that you will bail out on your marriage all by yourself. The devil cannot steal your gifts, so he will steal your joy of using your gifts, and you will disqualify yourself. The devil has no authority to steal your ministry, so he will steal the joy of your ministry, and you'll bail out on it yourself. Get the picture? **The devil practices subterfuge and sabotage.** Scripture says, "Run your race to win" (1 Cor. 9:24, *TLB*). But make no mistake, the devil will—with whispers of subterfuge and sabotage—lament to you on how long the race is, how tiring it is and how little you'll get out of it. Soon you'll slow down, thinking, *What am I getting out of serving so hard? I don't need this!* You'll disqualify yourself. The only one cheering will be the devil.

> *When the devil makes his move, God sounds the alarm. Listen for it and heed its wail. It could save your life and your destiny.*

The Bible warns us that the devil is "the accuser of our brethren" (Rev. 12:10) and "the father of lies" (John 8:44). Don't listen to him. He will set his sights to steal, kill and destroy your life, your future, your family and your ministry. Why? Because it's his insidious way to get back at our Savior who defeated him on the cross. It's his only chance at revenge—to hurt God by getting to His children.

Some years ago, Randolph Hearst, the newspaper magnate, was well known for his wealth and influence. Criminals knew it was virtually impossible to get to Hearst in order to access his wealth. Instead, they kidnapped his daughter Patty Hearst. Holding her for ransom, they finally were able to get to the one who controlled the wealth of the estate.

The same tactic is used by the archenemy of our families and futures. Satan can't get back at the One who holds the keys to sin and death. He can't retaliate against the King who defeated him at Calvary. Therefore, he entraps God's children—His sons and daughters who are called by His name! But when Satan makes his move, God sounds the alarm. Listen for it and heed its wail. It could save your life and your destiny.

3. When Acquiring Your Dream Requires Compromise

You may be entering a relationship that you know God would not approve. The Bible says, "Do not be yoked together with unbelievers" (2 Cor. 6:14, *NIV*). You know that, but you say, "Oh, but he's such a hunk! And I know he loves me."

> *Many things are worse than defeat, and compromise with evil is one of them.*
>
> —ANONYMOUS

If it's not something God would put His seal of approval on, then you need to seriously rethink that relationship. If you are married and feel you are falling in love with another woman, sirens should be blaring. Your marriage will be compromised and so will your faith. Just fast-forward this illicit scenario and you'll see how complicated your life will become.

Everything in your life needs to have God's seal of approval—absolutely everything. Acquire possessions, resolve problems and get your needs met the right way, because when you do, you allow God's very best to come to pass in your life:

> It is the blessing of the LORD that makes rich, and He adds no sorrow to it (Prov. 10:22).

If you want Bible blessings, do it the Bible way. God's blessings come with no sorrows. Don't wait until you've allowed your life to get so complicated that you're at the point of exasperation. God will give you early warning signals to alert you to choices that are out of His will far in advance. If you see any of these popping up on your radar screen—when close relationships suffer, when your joy diminishes or when you begin to compromise—*stop!*

> *If you want Bible blessings, do it the Bible way.*

Make some course corrections. It may save your life, and it will definitely restore simplicity, honesty and freedom.

The Principle of Margins

> Woe to those who add house to house and join field to field, until there is no more room, so that you have to live alone in the midst of the land! (Isa. 5:8).

One reason you may live in such complexity is because you are living a marginless life. Crowdedness creeps in unnoticed and grows like aggressive ground cover till it takes over your life and demands your allegiance. It usually begins with noble aspirations like building a better life for you and your family. It can come attached to the trophies of success or a promotion, causing you to feel obligated to spend more time to justify your increase. *Margins depict the space between your load and your limit.* If the load you are carrying is 80 pounds and your absolute limit is 100 pounds, then you have a 20 percent margin. If you are carrying 100 pounds when your limit is 100 pounds, then you are marginless or at capacity.

The same is true with money and budgeting. If you make $100 and you spend $50, you have a margin of 50 percent. If you make $100 and spend $150, you have debt.

A life without margins is a mother who is late for work, quickly straps her two-year-old son into his car seat and turns the key. The car wheezes and groans, and then gives up its meager attempts to start. Dead battery. The mother pounds the console in anger, spilling her coffee on her dress. She then turns around just in time to see her child throw up on his car seat.

The choice before us is plain: Christ or chaos, conviction or compromise, discipline or disintegration.

—PETER MARSHALL

Every book has margins. They are the white spaces around the edges of each page. I once measured the amount of blank space on a page and discovered an astounding revelation: 40 percent of the page was empty space. Now some can argue about how uneconomical and wasteful margins are: "Why, if we would run the words from one edge of the page to the other, we could cut the book by 20 pages, reduce the price and Lord knows how many trees we could save!" Maybe so. But who would read a book without margins? I wouldn't. (That's why I never read any of my college texts!)

No one begrudges a book its margins. Yet we live without them every day. We wonder why no one gets involved in our lives or ever reads our content. Relationships are hard to come by, and we find that our lives are sorely lacking in the department of close relationships.

One of the most important truths about margins is that friendships and acts of kindness are only built in the margins. Without them, we "live alone in the midst of the land." How can we build wider margins? Simple. Cut back. But cut wisely.

The Principle of Pruning

I will instruct you and teach you in the way which you should go; I will counsel you with My eye upon you. Do not be as the horse or as the mule which have no understanding, whose trappings include bit and bridle to hold them in check, otherwise they will not come near to you (Ps. 32:8-9).

Who is going to instruct and teach? Reread the very first word of the above Scripture. It says, "I." God says He will teach us and counsel us, directing our steps. He is willing to give us private lessons, personal counseling and individual help. That's absolutely amazing to me. His heart is willing to shape each of us individually and to guide us toward lives of fruitfulness and simplicity!

He also cautions us not to be like a stubborn horse or mule that requires bit and bridle. In other words, don't be like a stubborn animal that waits until the reins are pulled and then feels pain as the bit catches the top of the mouth, which *forces* the animal to pay attention and move in the right direction. I don't want you to be like that. Don't wait until you hit the wall. Don't wait until the pain is so great that you *have* to move just because of the pain. When you hear God's voice, prune to His instructions: "I will instruct you and teach you in the way which you should go."

Prune to God's Image

> "For I know the plans that I have for you," declares the
> LORD, "plans for welfare and not for calamity to give you
> a future and a hope" (Jer. 29:11).

The Bible says that God created you in His image (see Gen. 1:26). This means God had an image of you in His mind when He created you. Before you were born, God laid out the blueprint for your future. He is the master architect of your destiny. He has wonderful plans for you—plans for your family, your devotion, your faith and your ministry.

He created you and put a seed of that outstanding dream in you so that it would come to pass. The potential of that dream is in seed form inside you. Potential is untapped energy, unused strength and undeveloped gifts. You see, God's plans have already been deposited within you in the form of potential. There's only one catch: In order to fulfill your potential, you must partner and cooperate with God. Without your willingness, there is no relationship. It might be a dictatorship, like God's building obedient androids, but it wouldn't be a relationship. You are invited into a relationship with God. He "will instruct you and teach you in the way which you should go," but you have to do the "going," which requires your willingness to cooperate with His pruning and directives.

Turning potential into reality will require honesty about where you are. It will ask you for a willing-hearted compliance. If you come to church and you truly want to be the person God created you to be, then you must be willing to pray as David did:

> Search me, O God, and know my heart; try me and know
> my anxious thoughts; and see if there be any hurtful way
> in me, and lead me in the everlasting way (Ps. 139:23-24).

Get Real with God

I must *ruthlessly* root out any pretense, strip off any masks and be as honest as I can about my relationship with God. If we are the people of God, we need to have a minimal amount of pretending in our lives. Forget the Nielsen ratings; forget the congeniality contests. Let's get real with God.

I heard a story about a man who needed a job during an economic slump. It seemed that everybody else needed jobs too, so things started getting a little desperate. He was reading the classified ads and saw that the zoo was hiring, so he got in his car and zipped right over.

"I saw that the zoo is hiring! Is that true?" he inquired. "I can clean cages. I can greet visitors. Can I start there?"

The zookeeper said, "No, not really."

"I'll do anything. And I mean *anything.*"

"Well, uh," the zookeeper stammered, "let me tell you about the opening we have before you agree to do *anything.* Our favorite attraction here is our gorilla. And, well, our gorilla died yesterday, and we realize that without our gorilla, no one will come. We can't replace the gorilla right away, so we're looking for someone with some animation and theatrics background who will wear this fur suit and impersonate a gorilla until we can get a replacement."

Shocked, the man said, "Oh, no, no, no! I can't do that!"

"Nobody will know the difference," urged the zookeeper. "Just go in the cage and act like a gorilla."

"No, I don't think so," the man still protested.

"Well, it's the only job we have left."

With that said, the desperate job hunter finally agreed. He put on the gorilla suit and lumbered into the cage. He began with eating the peanuts

Oh, what a tangled web we weave, When first we practice to deceive!

—SIR WALTER SCOTT

and slowly graduated to hunching his back like a gorilla. Soon children wandering by stopped to watch. He noticed that the more "gorilla" he acted, the more excited the kids would get, so he started jumping and beating his chest. They loved it! A few more antics and soon dozens of curious onlookers crowded around the cage. He was the most popular exhibit in the entire zoo.

One day, he was swinging on his rope, doing aerial somersaults and working the crowd (as any normal gorilla would). Addicted to the adulations of the crowd, he swung himself higher and higher. Not realizing that the rope had frayed, he swung as far out as he could—and *snap!* The rope broke.

Now this one-part gorilla, two-parts ham sailed over his fenced area and landed flat on his back, right in the middle of his neighbor's property—the lion's den. Within a split second, a huge lion pounced on his chest, roaring loudly over his prey. "Help!" he yelled. "Help me somebody! I'm a human. I'm not really a gorilla. Someone get this lion off me before I get eaten alive. *Help!*"

At that moment, he heard a muffled voice from under the lion's mane, "Shut up, you fool, or we'll both get fired!"

I wonder how many times we come to church wearing rented "Christian" costumes. We put them on and everything looks fine, just fine. We look like Christians, we act like Christians, but on the inside, our families are falling apart or we know we're not living the way we're supposed to be. We know we're pretending in order to cover up what's really going on, yet we keep on pretending.

Let God Prune While You Cooperate

In so many words, God says, "I created you in My image, and anything that isn't My image, we will need to remove. I will point out those areas for you. I will sound the alarm when something foreign is beginning to become acceptable and normal. I will instruct you and teach you, but in order for you to receive My instruction, I will need your partnership. Come, follow Me."

I once watched a diamond cutter polish his gems. Under high-intensity lights and with the help of high-powered lenses, this master inspected each diamond for flaws or any

No pressure, no diamonds.

—MARY CASE

cloudiness in the stone. After careful cuts, he inspected it again. Periodically, he cut a diamond not just to facet the edges but also to remove any inherent flaw. Sometimes he put the nearly finished stone under a polishing machine and buffed the face of it in order to remove a scratch or any surface cloudiness.

The cutter's work continued until he was satisfied with the brilliance of the diamond. If a flaw did not polish out, he had no other choice but to cut the diamond into a smaller shape. If it still refused to polish out, his last resort was to crush it into fine particles to be used for sandpaper.

Our Father will refine us until the brilliance of His image is clearly seen without cloudiness or flaw. He will buff the surface of our lives until people see less of our face and more of His. However, if we, like a stubborn diamond, refuse to polish out, then we will be reduced to less than what our potential is. We will still be usable, but we will need to settle for a lesser role.

When God is working on an area of your life, be sure and polish out. Relinquish what He is attempting to remove. Don't stubbornly hold on to it. Don't excuse it or mask it. What is the secret of brilliance? Simply polish out what He points out as a flaw.

The Principle of the Sabbath

Remember the sabbath day, to keep it holy. Six days you shall labor and do all your work, but the seventh day is a sabbath of the LORD your God (Exod. 20:8-10).

A Sabbath is not an excuse for carnal laziness. It is holy. Taking time to be still is vital to restoring simplicity in our lives, because it renews, refreshes and refocuses us.

In other words, the Lord says to take one day out of seven and make it holy by not letting distractions cause you to violate it. A Sabbath is not an excuse for carnal laziness. It is holy. It is pleasing to God to see His children take time to be still. Taking time to be still is vital to restoring simplicity in our lives, because it renews, refreshes and refocuses us.

A Sabbath also reminds us that the world can go on without us. We are not the cat's meow. We are not indispensable. (I know this may be a rude awakening for some, but stick with me.) Taking a Sabbath is deemed holy, because it is an expression that recognizes God's sovereignty—that He, not we, holds all things together.

But I am afraid that, as the serpent deceived Eve by his craftiness, your minds will be led astray from the *simplicity and purity* of devotion to Christ (2 Cor. 11:3, emphasis added).

If we neglect our Sabbath and just keep on going, we begin to get caught up in the whirlpool of this world and its busyness, and we end up spinning around without direction. The Bible says that's what happened to Eve—she allowed her mind to be led astray from the "simplicity and purity" of walking with the Lord. God wants our relationship with Him to be something that is pure and simple. Anything other than that is not true devotion.

Pursuing a Pure and Simple Faith

If we allow ourselves to be led astray from a pure and simple walk with Jesus, we'll begin to see the damaging results. Our lives are too busy, and our marriages and families are falling apart. We often burn out much sooner on the inside than we do on the outside, and we feel burned-out much sooner than others see it.

It's the denial that exacerbates the damage. And it's not heeding God's early warning signs that causes the collapse.

How do we stop that from happening? The Bible says to stop and take a Sabbath. That's just one day out of seven. Rest, be still, and focus on God with one whole day out of every week.

To do great work a man must be very idle as well as very industrious.

—SAMUEL BUTLER

My weekly Sabbaths are on Mondays, since as a pastor I speak on the weekends. On Mondays, I often ride my motorcycle to the other side of the island, and I look forward to sitting at one of the panoramic lookout points.

One of my favorite spots overlooks beautiful Makapuu Bay. There I'll sit and enjoy a moment with the creator. I'll converse with the Lord and ask, "Lord, are we doing okay? Is there anything in my life that You need to prune? Is there anything in my thought life or attitudes? How am I doing with my family? Is there anything I need to change in my ministry? Search me, O God, and know my heart."

Those Sabbath moments are so critical in making my life simple enough to hear clearly what God is saying to me.

Taking Sabbath Moments Daily

Besides weekly Sabbaths, take Sabbath moments daily. I have a fairly large capacity that allows me to be committed to a lot of activities simultaneously. What keeps me sane, however, is sitting quietly before the Lord every single morning. I take my Bible, my journal and a cup of coffee, and I make time to hear God. Those daily Sabbath moments are so rich for me. They are times to recalibrate my life. I allow the Word of God to prune and adjust me.

Even when we're doing well and bearing fruit, we'll still hear the sound of pruning shears:

> Every branch in Me that does not bear fruit, He takes away; and every branch that bears fruit, *He prunes it* so that it may bear more fruit (John 15:2, emphasis added).

God is always working. Why? Because you have not arrived yet! It doesn't matter how many accolades you've received, you're not done yet. No matter how successful you may think you are, you're not home yet. Don't get so enamored with your gifts that you fall into the deception that you are indispensable. And don't get so wrapped up with how fruitful you are that you think you're invincible: "Let him who thinks he stands take heed that he does not fall" (1 Cor. 10:12).

Here are three great reasons why you need to take a Sabbath moment daily:

1. It restores your *faith*. "The LORD is my shepherd, I shall not want. He makes me lie down in green pastures; He leads me beside quiet waters. *He restores my soul*" (Ps. 23:1-3, emphasis added).

Have you ever needed your soul restored? Sure. We all have. But sometimes your shepherd has to make you lie down to receive it.

However, restoring your soul does not simply mean getting more physical rest. You can get a good night's sleep, but it won't necessarily restore your soul. You can wake up the next morning well rested and still have a weary soul. You can go to work, but your soul will not be in it. You can be a mom, but your soul is no longer in your responsibilities. You can be a minister or an elder, but your soul is absent from your duties.

Sabbath moments help you to fix your eyes on Jesus. And when you see Him, the problems return to their normal size.

At funerals, I often hear the phrase, "Let's pray for the departed soul of our loved one." I was recently thinking, *There are a lot of people I know in the Church who are still living, but their souls have departed, just like this dead person's! The activity still remains, but their souls have long departed.*

There's only One who can restore your soul—God. Take the time to spend Sabbath with Him. Your decision to do that is called "holy."

2. It restores your *focus*. Taking Sabbath moments can help you restore your focus. It can help you get your eyes off the waves and back on the One who walks on them. Sabbath moments help you fix your eyes on Jesus, "the author and perfecter of faith" (Heb. 12:2). When you see Him, the problems that were once exaggerated now return to their normal size. Taking Sabbath moments helps you magnify the Lord rather than

Only one thing has to change for us to know happiness in our lives: where we focus our attention.

—GREG ANDERSON

the problems. It makes life simple again.

There's a wonderful hymn that says:

Turn your eyes upon Jesus,
Look full in His wonderful face,
And the things of earth will grow strangely dim
In the light of His glory and grace.[2]

3. It restores your *flame*. Sabbath moments have the power to warm your heart and rekindle your first love for Jesus. Why? Because you tend to leave your first love.

At first you fall in love and you're inspired to give God your everything. In your innocence, you pour your heart into your serving, giving, helping, devotion and worship. But somewhere along the way, the exuberant flame slowly fades.

What God does is He restores your first love. That way you're not just doing things; rather, you're doing them out of a fullness of heart. You're not just raising your kids; you're doing it with a heart for parenting. You're not just married; you're married with a heart for your spouse. You're not just at home; you're home with a heart to be with your family. God restores the flame so that you have a heart for what He's called you to do and to be.

Only love makes me remember, it alone stirs my heart.

—LEONARDO DA VINCI

How do you make life simple again? It's simple. Maintain a Sabbath without violation. Guard your one day of rest, or those daily moments of restoration, and you'll see that, indeed, God will restore your soul. Don't feel guilty for taking a Sabbath. God says it is "holy."

Slow the world down a little bit. Get simple again. When you do, you'll see the beauty of His original design emerging in your reality.

Created in His Image

There once was a sculptor who began to chisel the form of Abraham Lincoln from a huge piece of granite. Every evening, after the sculptor chiseled the massive stone, a cleaning lady would come to sweep up the dust and debris. Day after day she would sweep up after him. Days turned into weeks, and weeks turned into months. Every day she saw the image emerge from the rock. Finally, the sculptor put the last polishing touches on what had become a magnificent, larger-than-life monument of Abraham Lincoln.

The day of the unveiling arrived. The sculpture was draped with a velvet cloth. Distinguished guests from around the nation were invited. To honor his cleaning lady, the sculptor invited her as his personal guest. The lights came on, the cameras were poised, and the veil was lifted. Gasps of "oohs" and "aahs" broke out as the crowd beheld the polished masterpiece of Abraham Lincoln.

As the evening came to a close, and the crowd slowly dwindled, only two people were left—the sculptor and the cleaning lady. He stood beside her as she gazed in amazement at the statue. He asked, "Well, what do you think?"

"This is magnificent! It is just magnificent!" she said with hushed awe. "I only have one question."

"What's that?" he said.

"How did you know that Mr. Lincoln was inside that rock?"

He paused and thought about the seemingly whimsical question. "You know," he replied, "I really didn't sculpt Mr. Lincoln. I simply chipped away whatever *wasn't* Mr. Lincoln."

God's Image in You

Inside your life is God's image—His plan for you. You are filled with potential! God is beginning to chip away thoughts, habits, attitudes and lifestyles—pieces of granite that you're holding tightly. God is saying, "This has to go."

> *There are hints of glory in our lives that yearn for fulfillment.*
>
> —MACRINA WIEDERKEHR

"Oh, but I love it," you protest, holding on to a familiar flaw.

"No, I'm sorry," the master replies compassionately. "It will only reduce your value if it's not pruned. Although I love you just like you are, I love you too much to let you stay that way. Trust Me."

Simple truths are many times the most profound. Each one you've just read holds a promise "to prosper you and not to harm you . . . to give you hope and a future" (Jer. 29:11, *NIV*). Learn these, and you will find life returning to its God-ordained simplicity.

May you enjoy a life of fresh simplicity!

Notes

1. Barbara Bush (lecture, commencement, Wellesley College, Wellesley, MA).
2. Source unknown.

DEVELOPING
CONTENTMENT

We are constantly bombarded with promises of eternal happiness.

Oh, sure, they may come in the form of TV commercials, but, nonetheless, they promise boundless contentment. They lure us with the idea that we're only one product away from happiness. Trinkets are the answer!

It starts out innocently—perhaps the allure of a Happy Meal tempted you as a child and promised to buy you some happiness. Or maybe a game or toy promised hours of entertainment and plenty of popularity with friends. Research shows that advertisers are targeting our innocent youth—both teens and preteens—as they have the most disposable income of any generation for their age, which shows why this "trinket magic" begins very early.

> *Happiness does not depend on outward things, but on the way we see them.*
>
> —LEO TOLSTOY

Most of us chuckle, knowing that a Happy Meal can never buy someone happiness. But the joke may be on us. As we get older, our trinkets just become more expensive and complicated. Commercials for new cars, finer beauty products and bigger homes keep us thirsting for more.

False Advertising

Advertisements fly through the airwaves and dive-bomb us: "You're only one trinket, one product, one program away from success!" They hold up a product and tempt us alluringly: "Use me, and you'll look like her! Wear me, and you'll find the love of your life. Put me in your hair, and you'll revive your youth!" (I tried it. It doesn't work.)

Take, for instance, the array of diet products and programs that bombard everyone who struggles with the battle of the bulge. From the strictest diet program's motto—if it tastes good, spit it out—to the most lenient one—eat anything you want as long as it fits on our specially designed plate—the diet wars abound.

Pretty soon, it's no longer a simple product that makes us happy, so we move on to bigger ticket items, like the allure of an affair: "If I could just have this one affair. No one would ever know. Anyway, God forgives, right? Just let me buy in to this trinket of a relationship." Or maybe it's the temptation of a better job: "If I could just get *that* job, I could have more money and prestige. *Then* I'd be happy." For others, it's the dream of owning a certain possession—a car, jewelry or clothes, a business or a house.

Biblical Contentment

If you've complained in the last six months about your education, your abilities, your appearance, your finances, how busy you are, your boss or your age, then contentment is an issue for you.

Let's read what Paul has to say about contentment:

> I have learned how to get along happily whether I have much or little. I know how to live on almost nothing or with everything. *I have learned the secret of contentment. . . . I can do everything God asks me to with the help of Christ who gives me strength and power* (Phil. 4:11-13, *TLB*, emphasis added).

Paul says he "learned" to be content. *Contentment is a learned skill, not an ability that falls casually into your lap.* It is an attitude that needs to be purposefully practiced over a period of time. Like a person who develops the ability to sink a jump shot in a basketball game or to play piano in a concert, he or she has mastered that skill through hours of practice. Paul implies that contentment is not a result of circumstances; rather, it is the result of an intentional lifestyle. Contentment is an inside job.

Everything has its wonders, even darkness and silence, and I learn, whatever state I may be in, therein to be content.

—HELEN KELLER

An Intentional Lifestyle

When Paul spoke about contentment, he did not mean we should simply accept the status quo. We're not supposed to listlessly lie down and take life as it comes, tolerating whatever happens. Neither did he intend that we settle into an attitude of resignation: *Que sera, sera*—"Whatever will be, will be"—or *C'est la vie*—"That's life!" Paul meant that *contentment is a skill we must cultivate*, no matter what.

Does the person with $10 million have more contentment than someone who has 10 children? The correct answer is no. The millionaire has less contentment, because he or she always wants more, while anyone with 10 children usually doesn't want any more.

> *An attitude of contentment means not being driven by always wanting more.*

Like the southern lady who had her first child and named him Eeny, had a second child and named him Meeny, had a third child and named him Miney and then had a fourth child and named him George. A neighbor asked, "Honey, why'd you name your kids Eeny, Meeny, Miney and then George?"

The four-time mom answered, "Cuz, I don't want no mo!"

Howard Hughes, the world-famous billionaire, once was asked, "You have so much money! How much is enough?"

His answer? "Just a little bit more."

Just a Little Bit More

You can buy a nice, new car but in a year or two want another. You can accumulate loads of money but still want more and more. You can become addicted to possessions, but when is enough ever enough? Like a drug, *increasing how much we consume only increases how much more we want!*

On the other hand, contentment is freedom. It's freedom from dissatisfaction, out-of-control appetites and the itch you can never quite scratch. It's freedom from the times you find yourself thinking, *I gotta have it! I can't live without it!* Contentment is the salve that soothes and frees you.

A few years ago, there was a commercial for Nestea Iced Tea, called "The Nestea Plunge." The commercial opened with a guy lifting up a glass of iced tea. Little beads of water trickled slowly down the side of the glass. The weather was sweltering hot. The guy dripped with perspiration and next to him was a swimming pool. He took a drink from the frosty glass and experienced such total contentment that he fell backward into the cool pool. As he fell, he said with a satisfied smile, "Aah!"

> *We must all suffer one of two pains: the pain of discipline or the pain of regret. The difference is discipline weighs ounces while regret weighs tons.*
>
> —JIM ROHN

Stop and say the word, "Aah." Pause, relax, and say it again with a deep sense of satisfaction, "Aah." That's what contented people say.

"Aah!"

Practice contentment and say, "Aah," over this next week. When you say "Amen," try it the contented way: "Aah-men." When you sit down to eat the dinner that your spouse has cooked for you, say, "Aah! This is wonderful." When you climb into your old rust bucket that is parked next to a gleaming Mercedes-Benz, just say, "Aah." Then, as you and your rust bucket are jammed in traffic, find a nice radio station, lean back and say, "Aah." As you arrive home and put the key in the lock of your little house, causing the door to fall off its hinges, just say, "Aah, this door is so easy to open now!"

> *The way we see the problem is the problem.*
>
> —STEPHEN COVEY

For the next week, whatever happens to you, remind yourself to say, "Aah!" That way you'll develop new "Aah-ttitudes." Practice these "Aah-ttitudes" apart from your circumstances and apart from what you think gives you contentment. You'll be amazed at the garden of contentment that will begin to sprout all around you.

As you practice your newfound contentment, let's look at three helpful keys for learning the secret of fulfillment. These three keys will serve to remind you to say, "Aah!" Notice that each one contains the word, "Aah," just to get you warmed up and practicing your new "Aah-ttitudes."

1. Learn "Aah" Right View of Problems

Life is like a tube of toothpaste. You don't know what's inside until it's been squeezed!

Contentment is not the result of an absence of problems. Problems are inevitable. Why? Because we live in an imperfect world that's filled with imperfect people—two of those include you and me! We're also married to imperfect people, and they married us. Therefore, problems come as part of the package. How can we have a godly view of them?

Problems Are Inevitable; Rebuilding Is a Choice

Problems don't necessarily build character. Problems *reveal* character. You decide what to do with the findings. You can react with blame, anger, discouragement or denial—all of these are less than desirable if you want to rebuild. Or you can realize your shortcomings and begin the rebuilding process.

One of our church's core values addresses this squarely. It states that we will not give audience to complaining; instead, we will courageously face each problem in a way that honors God and builds biblical character. One of the best ways to face problems is to address them as the Lord would address them. Isn't that great?

Because God is a God of redemption and restoration, everything He touches changes. Nothing He touches can remain the same. Therefore, whenever you speak of problems, always speak of them as changing. This will give you a hopeful light at the end of a darkened tunnel. It's also a positive indicator that you are in the process of growing.

If someone tells you, "Boy, you've got financial problems!" and you respond, "Man, do I ever have financial problems! I have always had financial problems. I will always have financial problems. And until the day I die, I think I am going to have financial problems!" your response doesn't offer any light or any hope. However, if someone says, "You have a financial problem," and you respond, "Yes, I do, but it's *changing!*" your response introduces an element of hope, turning a problem into a growth opportunity.

Got a Problem? "Yes, but It's Changing!"

When someone points out that you have a bad marriage, quickly say, "Yeah, but it's changing." Or when they remind you that you blew your test really badly, you correct them and say, "Yeah, but it's changing!" And if someone tells you that you've got bad breath, you speak right to them and say, "Yeah, but it's changing!"

The first key in learning the secret of contentment is simple: Whenever you speak of problems, speak of them as changing. It will allow you to develop a new perspective and a fresh view of your problems. You will be able to see your problems in the right light, not allowing your eyes to remain focused on them. You will see where Jesus is working. And you'll be able to genuinely and confidently say, "Aah-men!"

2. Learn to Cultivate "Aah" Grateful Heart

In *everything* give thanks; for this is God's will for you in Christ Jesus (1 Thess. 5:18, emphasis added).

We must learn to cultivate a grateful heart in "everything"—not just when perfect gifts are delivered at our doorstep, but also when imperfect gifts arrive uninvited.

> *Gratitude is the heart's money.*
>
> —FRENCH PROVERB

It's easy to be thankful for good gifts, but how do we cultivate gratefulness for bad gifts? Now that's something we need to work on. Remember, life is like a garden: It only grows what we cultivate. Gratefulness will never bloom until we cultivate it in the soil of our lives.

If you are waiting for perfect gifts to incite gratefulness, then you'll wait your whole life. Waiting for the perfect life, the perfect job, the perfect mate or the perfect pastor will always leave you suffering from a low-grade fever of discontent and frustration. Don't wait for a grateful heart, initiate it!

Gratefulness at Your Fingertips

Imagine yourself as a person in training, learning to practice gratefulness in your imperfect world. How can you possibly do it? Let me tell you one easy way that will make a world of difference: Tell yourself, "I am going to be grateful!" Then *practice* gratefulness.

Remember that imperfect spouse you have? Some of you may need to say to your spouse, "I am grateful that I'm married to you," even though on the inside you're thinking, *No way!* Or those imperfect kids you

> *Gratitude unlocks the fullness of life.*
>
> —MELODY BEATTIE

have? They may need to hear you say, "I'm so grateful for you!" It may drop their jaws, but they'll love it. Remember that boss of yours? Maybe it's about time you said something nice to him or her, too: "I'm grateful for my job, and I'm grateful that you're my boss." It may just rejuvenate your workplace. You're not saying that person is the perfect boss or you work in a perfect environment. You are not looking for perfections as much as you are practicing gratefulness. Practice little acts of gratefulness every day.

As Seen on TV

Often the reason why we cannot cultivate a grateful spirit is because we hate reality. We have grown up in a virtual world in which it is considered better to view life through the Technicolor wonders of television.

It's easy to see why we're so captivated when we watch the amazing video technology that goes into a 30-second commercial. Millions of dollars go into hiring the advertising companies, camera people, makeup artists, models, actors and writers.

Then after they're all done shooting, the job has only just begun. Next, they transform the commercial using the modern-day wizardry of computer technology—a blemish erased here, a Hawaiian sunset dropped there. Hours upon hours of experts and brushups later, this 30-second epic is finally ready to air on prime-time TV.

Not Just Good, Hollywood Good

The media does a great job of focusing on the most exciting, titillating things, even if they have to create fabrications. If things get a little ho-hum or normal, they cut to something that's wildly exciting and entertaining. That way, we keep watching and advertisers keep making money, as we buy into their promises of perfect, exciting lives.

Compared to the beautiful people with ever-exciting lives, new clothes, perfect hair and flawless skin, our lives suddenly look drab. We start to think, *Well, I don't have a shiny new car that's a babe magnet. And my wife isn't the high school cheerleader she was when I first met her. Our kids aren't as funny as those witty TV kids. Hey! Why is my life so boring?*

> *Besides learning to see, there is another art to be learned—not to see what is not.*
>
> —MARIA MITCHELL

Ever feel that way? Especially after viewing an entire sitcom or a glamorous magazine full of glossy advertisements? Suddenly you look at your life and it's just not the same.

The Not-So-Glamorous Life

It is like those glamour-shot photography sessions: Anybody in the world can walk in and be transformed into a supermodel. A photographer takes your picture and out you go with glossy 8 x 10s of you as a cover model.

First, stylists mold your hair in place using three cans of hair spray. To get it into the right proportions, they pull all of your hair from behind your head to the front. "Needs more body!" they shout, as they keep pulling every single strand up to the front. Of course, you'll never see the backside, because it resembles the backside of a turkey.

Now that your hair is just right (it looks like those big billowing storm clouds right before the thunder and lightning strikes), they begin to work on your face. Several pounds later of foundation, concealer and powder, your face feels like papier-mâché. But they still have to define your features—on goes the eyeliner, eye shadow, blush, lip liner and lipstick. They then take great pleasure in tweezing off your eyebrows and then drawing them back on. (And that's just for guys!)

It's the most heinous process and completely degrading—all to make you look like a superstar. But in reality, you're just a normal, everyday person who pays extra for an "image" of someone "better." Is that even logical?

Perhaps you've grown up with expectations of life that often don't match reality. But when reality shows up like an unexpected bill, you get upset. You don't like reality. You prefer to live with your fantasy-inspired expectations.

That attitude is often the precursor of danger in a marriage. You walk to the altar and say, "I do," to an *expectation* of a husband or an *expectation* of a wife. You only see the glamorous front of this person, which represents your expectation of what you want this person to be. That's why this stage of relationships is called "attraction," because you put your best face forward. You marry someone who symbolizes your ideal, picture-perfect mate. However, soon enough, your expectations evaporate in the harsh light of reality. You get a flash of the real, behind-the-scenes person. You catch a glimpse of the backside of the makeover, and you're left singing the blues: "Is that all there is?"

There's a simple rule in life that says that contentment equals reality minus expectations:

Contentment = Reality - Expectations

The Real World

We need to enjoy the reality of who people are—personality, blemishes and all. "The good, the bad and the ugly," as one general put it. We need to learn to live with reality and not with fantastic expectations. This releases people to be themselves—who God created them to be. It also allows you and me to be ourselves.

> *True happiness is not attained through self-gratification but through fidelity to a worthy purpose.*
>
> —HELEN KELLER

Once we start accepting people just as they are, we get to relax and be grateful for God's creation. We all get to be real! I have found that I work the hardest at improving myself when I first know that I am loved and accepted just as I am.

With the first two "Aahs" in developing an attitude of contentment in place, we're well on our way to growing our garden of contentment. There's just one more key to discovering the secret of contentment.

3. Stake Your Life on What Satisfies "Aah" Soul

Your life is eternally precious. Be sure that you invest it wisely. The only wise investment is in what satisfies your soul. Don't waste your life chasing trinkets that never make you happy. This is so important, I can't emphasize it enough—even Jesus reminded us of this life-impacting secret:

> Do not worry, saying, "What shall we eat?" or "What shall we drink?" or "What shall we wear?" For . . . your heavenly Father knows that you need them. But *seek first his kingdom and his righteousness,* and all these things will be given to you as well (Matt. 6:31-33, *NIV,* emphasis added).

Jesus points to the one thing we should seek after with everything we've got. It's the only thing that can give us ultimate fulfillment: *"his kingdom and his righteousness."* Only *then* can all these things be added to us.

In other words, Jesus is saying contentment cannot be acquired directly. Rather, *contentment is a by-product of a life focused on God.* He is the One and only focal point that will truly satisfy our

> *You nourish your soul by fulfilling your destiny.*
>
> —RABBI HAROLD KUSHNER

souls. Content people are those whose aim in life is much bigger than attaining mere contentment.

"Aah" Is the Ultimate Fulfillment

If your sole aim is to acquire possessions and money, contentment will be as elusive as a butterfly. You'll chase after it your whole life.

On the other hand, Jesus says that if you really want to stake your life on what will satisfy your soul, then follow His purposes for your life. It is then that He will add contentment to you.

Ask those who have given their lives for the gospel, sacrificing much and living lives for the kingdom of God. You will hear and see how content they are. Their lives are aimed at a much larger goal than mere contentment.

Contentment Is an Inside Job

Some of you are suffering in your marriage. You want very much to experience God's promises in your life together as husband and wife. However, you're married to a partner who doesn't share that desire. Yet Paul said, "I have learned to be content whatever the circumstances" (Phil. 4:11, *NIV*). *Contentment is not determined by what you have—whether it's a lot or a little. Contentment is determined by the set of your heart.* It's an attitude—one that has to be learned. Contentment is an inside job.

Some people might say, "Paul didn't know what he was talking about. He doesn't know the marriage I'm in. He doesn't know my yearning for a child when I can't have one. He doesn't know the things I go through with chronic pain. Paul doesn't know anything about my suffering."

Actually, Paul didn't live a cushy, aristocratic life. He really did know what it meant to have little. He was often hungry. Paul was alone and abandoned. He was stoned, shipwrecked, whipped, beaten and left for dead. Paul was someone who had been mocked, lied about, ridiculed and slandered. Most of Paul's words were probably written in chains. Paul knew exactly what he was talking about when he said, "I have learned the secret of being content in any and every situation" (v. 12, *NIV*), and it probably had nothing to do with having chains or not having chains.

When Paul wrote his famous words about contentment, he was writing them from prison.

Contentment Is Freedom

Paul understood contentment. As he was writing those words, he was facing the possibility of torture and death. Within a few years, he would indeed be tortured to death. How in the world could he talk about contentment? His aim in life was much bigger than contentment itself.

Paul's aim was to know God and to serve Him with all his heart, not to attain a lifestyle of convenience and comfort. His desire was that his life would somehow, in some way, be used to bring God's purposes to pass. This attitude was what caused contentment to flood into his life.

Contentment Is Humility

Our goal should be to attain a Paul-like attitude. To Paul, everything of this world faded because he found something that really mattered. He humbled himself and most likely said, "Lord, here's my life. Use it for Your purposes and Your desires."

Sometimes we Christians can be very discontent. We live frustrated lives because we are going after our own contentment. We seem just like people who don't know Jesus. The only difference is that they use skills and maneuvering. *We do it much more discreetly—we use God.*

We treat God as if He were a genie in a magic lamp, trying to rub Him the right way. Three wishes become unlimited prayers, and instead of wriggling our noses or wishing our way through our lists,

We pray, too often, not to do God's will, but to enlist God's assistance in maintaining our "continually increasing consumption."

—JOY DAVIDMAN

we simply pray for bigger paychecks, bigger homes, more prestige, more influence or more possessions. In essence, we're saying, "God,

I want You to help *me* fulfill *my* purposes for *my* life. That is the source of *my* contentment: Your fulfilling *my* desires."

Contentment is still the name of the game. We just pray for it in Jesus' name.

Aim Higher

When we aim at something bigger than contentment, we say, "Lord, here's my life. Use it for Your purposes and Your desires. Whatever I have—skills, finances, relationships and time—I lay them at Your feet. How can I use them? Instruct me so that I can be a faithful steward. Whether I have much or little, I will be content knowing You are using my life. Come, Lord, live Your life through me."

All of a sudden, God says, "Because you are seeking first the kingdom of God and His righteousness, I will give you contentment." *Contentment is a by-product of living a life according to God's will.* Only then does contentment become something we reach and not an elusive desire that always escapes our grasp.

Desperately Seeking Something

We can be like the billionaire who wanted to fly the fastest airplane in the world. But in order to do so, he had to design, build and pilot it. He also wanted to have boats and expansive estates and live in exotic places. So he bought these things. He amassed such a great fortune that he had two United States presidents at his bidding. He believed he could get more and more contentment by having more sexual encounters, more expeditions, more explorations and more excursions. And that's just what he did.

Basing our happiness on our ability to control everything is futile.

—STEPHEN COVEY

Fast-forward the tape to the end of his life. His hair was long and unkempt, his beard was disheveled, and his fingernails resembled pale yellow corkscrews. He had purchased a large hotel and lived there in self-imposed solitary confinement. Bedridden, he would sit in a drug-induced trance peering at life from his dark, sunken eyes and emaciated body. His arms were filled with the puncture marks of a drug addict who frantically attempted to jab contentment into his veins.

He died in a very lonely pit of despair, trapped in a hollow skeletal shell. He had missed life itself.

I am sure you will recognize the name of this sad billionaire: Howard Hughes. Though he had billions of dollars and the world at his fingertips, he was never content. For all of his achievements and endeavors, Howard Hughes left only a sad legacy. He is known as a man who lived his whole life searching for contentment but never found it.

> *When asked how much money would be enough, billionaire Howard Hughes answered, "Just a little bit more."*

Contentment Beyond Measure

On the other hand, if you had asked Mother Teresa if she was content in her abject poverty and simple life, you would have gotten a different response. If you ask millions of Christians who serve God with all of their hearts, suffering in the name of Christ, they will echo her response. Their answer is: contentment beyond measure. Regardless of whether they have a little or a lot, they find the greatest reward in seeking God and His kingdom. Contentment is an inside job.

Psalm 65:4 provides a closer insight to this secret of satisfaction:

How blessed is the one whom You choose and *bring near to You* to dwell in Your courts. We will be satisfied with the goodness of Your house, Your holy temple (emphasis added).

What satisfies our souls? *Being near to the Lord!* We can be Christians, but if we are not near to the Lord, it will be a dissatisfying experience. You can be a mother, but if you are not near to the Lord, it will be a dissatisfying experience. You can be an elder or a pastor in a church, but if you are not near to the Lord, it will still be dissatisfying. Draw near to Him and you'll notice a pizzazz, a sparkle, an eternal contentment to every role you happily fulfill.

"Aah-men!"

As you go through your day, even now, make a note to *practice contentment* and *practice gratefulness*. When you eat dinner, regardless of what is set before you, you have an opportunity to open up and say, "Aah." When you are sitting in your car, stopped in traffic, you have an opportunity to sit back, tune in to some nice music, listen, enjoy and say, "Aah." Most important, when you are done praying, don't just quickly mumble, "Amen"; instead, take the opportunity to say "Aah-men!"

Contentment is an inside job.

Contentment is an inside job, a skill that must be learned. Learn these three essential "Aahs," and you'll be rewarded with "Aah" life that rises "Aah-bove!"

BUILDING THE COURAGE TO REBUILD

His name is Lee Capps. He should be dead today.

Some time ago, he took off from a Washington airfield with a pilot friend in a small Cessna airplane. It was just the two of them out for a spin. When they got to cruising altitude, his friend suddenly had a massive heart attack and died.

Capps had one other problem. He had never flown an airplane before in his life.

Mustering all the resolve he could, Capps pulled his friend off the controls, grabbed the microphone and desperately cried out for help.

An air traffic controller heard his distress call and tried to calm him down. In soothing tones, he said, "Okay, I'm an air traffic controller, and I can hear you just fine." Then to inject

We admit defeat, not when we are knocked down, but when we refuse to get back up!

some humor into a desperate situation, he continued, "I understand you might be having a problem up there. Well, I have some good news for you. I'm also a flight instructor. Would you be interested in a lesson?"

"Tell me everything you know—and do it now!" Capps fired back.

The air traffic controller gave Capps the fundamentals of flying an aircraft and a few instructions on steering, as well a how-to lesson on stabilizing the plane. Finally, the air traffic controller said, "Well, Lee, now comes your final exam. You will have to apply everything you have just learned. You're going to have to attempt a landing. It's your only hope."

The flight instructor walked him through the landing procedure step-by-step. First, he instructed Capps to align the plane with the runway. Then he talked him through the procedure of dropping altitude in order to begin his approach. As you can imagine, it wasn't the most graceful approach. The plane looked like a drunken goose trying to find its way home. But with the systematic coaching, Capps finally landed the plane and miraculously walked away with only minor injuries.

By this time, reporters had swarmed in for the unbelievable story. One of them interviewed the air traffic controller. "Did you really think Lee Capps had a shot at landing that plane? What were the odds?"

The air traffic controller looked him square in the eye and said, "I knew it was a long shot, and all the odds were stacked against him, but Lee Capps defied all the odds, and he's alive today!"

Defying the Odds

There are a lot of people like Lee Capps who defy the odds. For some, defying the odds is a lifestyle, a career and even a sport.

There are all kinds of ways people try to defy the odds. Stockbrokers, to some extent, defy the odds, as do actuaries. Life insurance salespeople can tell you the precise numerical odds of living to the ripe old age of 92. Those who sell car insurance think that way all the time. These people are professionals in using probability formulas. They can tell you that there is a 10 times greater chance that you will get in an accident on a bicycle than in an automobile. They also can

For a righteous man falls seven times, and rises again.

—PROVERBS 24:16

tell you that you have a greater chance of ending up in an accident driving a sports car than a family van. They also estimate that if you drive a Honda Civic, there is a 57 percent greater probability you will have it stolen than if you drive a Dodge Dart. Makes sense!

Others play the odds in Las Vegas. It seems like half of Hawaii flies to Las Vegas and deposits its economy in their slot machines.

There are plenty of extreme sports that titillate, tickle and dare people to defy the odds. Some bungee jump. Others risk their lives in survivor games. There is a new sport in which the daring (or dumb, depending on your sanity) hop into an airplane and fly over snow-covered mountain passes with a snowboard strapped to their feet. When they find the right spot, they launch themselves out of the plane, hit the side of the slopes and snowboard down the mountain.

When the Odds Are Against You

Many people live day to day feeling like the odds are stacked against them. Some of us have lost hope along the way. We've lost faith in the possibility that a long shot will ever happen in our lives. What do you do when you have to look up to see the bottom? What do you do when you need courage to rebuild? What do you do when your life is in ruins—you've lost relationships, you've lost face, and you've lost possessions?

When things crumble and come crashing down, God's people can find new strength to rise above rather than living life beneath the rubble. Proverbs 24:16 says: "For a righteous man falls seven times, and rises again." The righteous ones find the courage to rebuild again and again.

The Bible is replete with examples of people who rose again to rebuild. Job's entire estate and family were destroyed. Moses was disinherited by Pharaoh, his name scratched off the annals of Egyptian history. Joseph was betrayed by his brothers and sold into slavery. Even the apostle Paul was convicted as a serial killer. To the casual observer, Paul looked like a long shot. But through this one man, God brought about half of the New Testament while he was incarcerated in prison. David sinned with Bathsheba and murdered her husband. Peter denied the Lord. Mary Magdalene was a woman riddled with personal demons. Yet God's strength caused each of these individuals to defy the odds.

> *Success is never found. Failure is never fatal. Courage is the only thing.*
>
> —WINSTON CHURCHILL

Have you ever felt destroyed, disinherited or sold out? The story's not over yet! You have a chance to rebuild just like these biblical believers did by following three key foundational principles for rebuilding.

1. Make Peace with God

Before we go any further, we need to get one thing perfectly clear: The goal of rebuilding must be to make peace with God. It's not primarily to get back with certain people (e.g., a spouse or an ex), and it's not to regain possessions or recover our reputation. Rather, our first goal in rebuilding is a matter of the heart:

> When a man's ways are pleasing to the LORD, He makes even his enemies to be at peace with him (Prov. 16:7).

The cry of your heart must be to please God alone. When you make the goal of your heart to please God, then He is released to restore your relationships, your reputation and your life. The Bible tells us that when this happens, even your enemies will be at peace with you. Any other motivation becomes a lame attempt to see God as your private banker—your genie in a lamp. If your motivation is to regain a relationship or to restore your estate, then your prayers will more likely resemble a deal you are trying to negotiate with God: "Lord, please save me from this bankruptcy thing. I swear, if You help me get out of this one, I'll never waste money again. I'll even start tithing!"

You never want your times with God reduced to deal-making sessions. Jesus once told those who were buying and selling in the Temple: "Stop making My Father's house a place of business" (John 2:16).

Although you're not buying and selling sacrificial animals, you can turn your times with God into negotiations for bigger deals when you seek only what you want. Rather, seek to repair relationships. Let your primary goal simply be to make peace with God. He'll start first with remedying you, as a person, rather than your situation. He will begin by restoring the missing character that may have caused the collapse in the first place. Why? Because absent or faulty character will result in a crash, and if you don't rebuild correctly, you will fall victim to repeating the same mistakes over and over again.

> *Rebuilt character makes room for renewed wisdom.*

Rebuilt character makes room for renewed wisdom. Whenever God extends forgiveness, He also extends wisdom. Forgiveness and wisdom come hand in hand. Just take them!

After his fifth marriage, a forlorn man asked me, "Why don't my marriages ever work out? I've had five women, and none of them ever seemed to be able to get her act together!"

If your heart doesn't change, neither will the scenery.

The Starting Point

A young acolyte once interrogated an old preacher with some barbed queries: "Why isn't there any revival in today's churches? What's wrong with the churches? What's wrong with *this* church? Maybe it's the people's stubbornness! Maybe it's the leaders!"

As this impetuous critic kept up his litany of accusations, the wise old preacher took a piece of chalk from a nearby blackboard and on the carpet he drew a circle around the young man.

"What in the world are you doing?" the young man asked.

The old preacher slowly replied, "When revival begins in this circle, then revival will begin in this church."

The first step begins with you. Make peace with God! This is foundational. Stop the blame game. Don't justify. Regardless of how wrong you think the other person is, start with your own heart. Psalm 139:23-24 gives us a revealing glimpse into David's heart and into the reason why God used him so greatly:

> *You must be the change you wish to see in the world.*
>
> —MAHATMA GHANDI

> Search me, O God, and know my heart; test me and know my anxious thoughts. See if there is any offensive way in me, and lead me in the way everlasting (*NIV*).

2. Be Obedience Oriented, Not Results Oriented

The second step in digging out from beneath the rubble is to make sure the dial of our hearts is set on *obedience* and not on *results*. When we're focused on results, we begin looking for immediate outcomes. We tend to take shortcuts and justify compromise. We start to match God's performance against our expectations, and we view God through the faulty spectacles of impatience.

The blessing of being obedience oriented is that you'll see every event as an opportunity to grow. You're no longer waiting for others to change. You've instead drawn the circle around yourself.

The primary question of someone seeking to be obedience oriented is not Why? Obedience does not insist on answers.

It does not require explanations to satisfy the demands with which we all struggle in times of calamity. Instead, the question is What? What do You want me to do? What do You want me to think? What do You want me to say?

The blessing of being obedience oriented is that you'll see every event as an opportunity to grow.

"Why" questions defy answers. "What" questions invite direction. When you ask "what" questions, you begin to resolve the issue. Asking what also reflects a heart that seeks God's counsel and submits in obedience. What a precious heart indeed!

If you want to defy the odds and live life above the rubble, take ownership of your life by being obedience oriented. It's a surefire secret to success, guaranteed by God.

3. Get a Clear Perspective from God

Ever notice that when life comes crashing down, everybody wants to give you an opinion? Like Job's counselors, everyone has a perspective of what you should do to get your life back in order. Suddenly everyone's an expert. But there's only one perspective that matters—*God's.*

God knows you better than you know yourself. The book of Jeremiah reminds us that He knew you before you were even fashioned in your mother's womb (see 1:5).

The best thing you can do (beyond listening to all of the well-meant advice you receive) is to go straight to the source. Check in with God and get a clear perspective of where you are in your life. If you seek His direction with an honest heart, God will reveal His viewpoint. Like viewing a city from a mountaintop, God will give you a lay-of-the-land perspective on your circumstance. That way, you will get to see how what you are experiencing fits with the rest of your life.

To change and to improve are two different things.

—GERMAN PROVERB

"You Are Here"

Have you ever been in a mall with multiple levels and cavernous superstores that seem to stretch on forever? We have one of those in Hawaii. If you get lost in one of those places, it would take the search-and-rescue team days to find you! Unsuspecting shoppers wanting to make a simple purchase are found mesmerized at the entrance level, faced with zillions of options beckoning them into consumer oblivion.

Fraught with fear of being lost for days, you find yourself at a lighted directory in the middle of one of the many thoroughfares. Desperate for simple directions, you scan the map and a large red arrow catches your attention. It reads, "You are here."

Hallelujah! What a relief! You are not lost. You are found! You find the store you want to shop at, see where it is in relation to where you are, and the rest is simple direction following.

What we learn from this geography lesson (albeit in a mall) is, *If you don't know where you are, how will you get to where you want to go?*

I once counseled a husband and wife. I asked the husband to sit outside for a minute so that I could ask his wife a question. I asked her, "On a pain scale of 1 to 10 (with 1 being defined as no pain and 10 as severe pain), how would you rate your marriage?"

With a cringe, she said, "Twenty-five!"

I then had her change places with her husband outside, and I asked him the exact same question. He answered, "Oh, probably 2 or 3."

The husband was living in la-la land, while his wife was at the end of her rope. He had no clue that the red arrow of his marriage was indicating "You are here."

Keeping a clear perspective of exactly where we are in God's eyes is crucial to navigating the rebuilding process. Otherwise, we'll get lost in the shuffle of cheap opinions and well-meaning advisers.

God's Viewpoint from Mount Perspective

Your word is a lamp to my feet and a light to my path (Ps. 119:105).

There is no better lookout point from which to view our life than the Bible. God's Word is so important, because it provides not only a healthy perspective but also God's perspective. Without His viewpoint, we may be dangerously close to the edge and not realize it. A slight nudge from an unsuspecting remark or comment and our world crashes in.

God's Word is the red arrow telling you, "You are here." His counsel instructs you in the way you should go. "Now that you know where you are, here's where I want you to be," He says, as His finger points to another area of the map.

Now you're ready to rebuild. Just follow the following three steps.

Step 1: Make a Decision to Rebuild

One of my favorite stories is about a personal hero of mine, Thomas Alva Edison. He invented the incandescent lightbulb and the automobile battery, and he pioneered the film industry. It's not just his creative intelligence I admire but also his tenacious spirit. Toward the autumn years of his life, he worked in a modest building that resembled an old barn. There with his son, Edison would work late into the night laboring diligently to perfect his inventions. One evening, in an attempt to improve the retention of a battery's charge, an unfortunate combination of chemicals caused his experiment to burst into flames. Flickering tongues of fire went licking and lapping up the side of the dry old barn. Within a few minutes, the whole barn was ablaze.

> *An optimist sees an opportunity in every calamity; a pessimist sees a calamity in every opportunity.*
>
> —WINSTON CHURCHILL

Edison's apprentice son ran out of the barn in time to see the 60-foot flames devour the entire building. Quickly realizing that his father was nowhere to be seen, he began to call out desperately for his father.

"Dad! Dad, get out of there!"

He feared that his father might be inside, going down with his precious life's work. "Dad!" he cried, as he frantically ran around the barn searching for any sign of his dad.

Just as he came around the corner for a third time, he almost ran headlong into his father whose hands were thrust deep in his pockets. Both his smock and white hair were now covered in a thick layer of black soot. He stood oblivious to it all, gazing intently at the flames.

"Dad! I was afraid you would go down with the flames," cried his son in sheer relief.

Without taking his eyes off the flames, Thomas Edison said, "Son, go get your mother!"

"But why, Dad?" asked the shocked son.

The senior Edison answered, "Because your mother comes from a very small town and she has never seen a fire like this!"

> *Genius is one percent inspiration and ninety-nine percent perspiration.*
>
> —THOMAS ALVA EDISON

After a couple more minutes, the whole barn was just a smoldering heap. When it had finally been reduced to ash, the legendary Edison turned to his son and asked, "Do you know anyone with a tractor?"

"Sure, Dad. A guy down the road has one. But why do you want it now?"

Edison said, "Because it's time to rebuild."

The Spark Plug of Motivation

When you look at people like Thomas Edison and others who pick themselves up from utter ruin, you have to wonder, *What is the source of their strength?*

Sift through the details of Edison's life story and you'll find the answer: *He made a decision to rebuild.* As you look at your own life, you *must* make that same decision. It all begins with a commitment to rebuild.

"But I don't have the courage," you protest. God says you don't have to look for courage:

> Have I not commanded you? Be strong and courageous! Do not tremble or be dismayed, for the LORD your God is with you (Josh. 1:9).

Courage is not a feeling you have to stir up. It's not an emotion you wait for. Courage is a command! It's an action that you take because you have been commanded to do so, regardless of whether your knees are knocking. It is a choice you make, not a feeling you wait for.

A good soldier understands commands. If he is ordered to "stand up," then regardless of how he feels, he stands up. He doesn't say, "Well, I don't really feel like standing up right now, sir."

God says, "I *command* you to be courageous." Your reply needs to be: "Yes, sir, I am courageous!" Your knees may be knocking and there may be butterflies in your stomach, but regardless of how you feel, you choose to be courageous!

> *Most of the important things in the world have been accomplished by people who have kept on trying when there seemed to be no hope at all.*
>
> —DALE CARNEGIE

Around and Around We Go

When I began in ministry many years ago, I was a youth leader in Youth for Christ. This ministry took us to high school lunchrooms where we made contacts with students.

I remember the first few times I went to visit. I was so scared to go onto campus that I drove in circles around the parking lot for one hour, and then I drove home. I was waiting for a bolt of courage to strike me, but I guess it wasn't the season. It wasn't until I said to myself, *Forget the feelings! I must start with the action,* that my ministry began to build.

Courage is not the absence of fear. Rather, courage is moving forward in spite of fear. You make a decision to go forward and walk as courageously as you can. Why? Because God says, "I *command* you."

If you're waiting around for the *feeling* of courage to come, it never will. Some people say, "I sing because I'm happy." I choose to sing regardless of the situation. In the midst of struggle, I'll sing, "How Great Thou Art." Why? Because He commands me to be strong and courageous no matter the circumstance.

You need to take your faith by the shoulders and shake it, saying, "I am going to rebuild." Although your emotions say, "I don't want to," you must remember God's words: "Have I not commanded you? Be strong and courageous! Do not tremble or be dismayed, for the LORD your God is with you."

Make a decision to rebuild. Nothing happens until you do. Otherwise, you'll take the path of least resistance. You'll look for justifications, shortcuts and side doors. Instead, be strong and very courageous!

Strength Follows Commitment

I remember one lethargic day when I was at home. Bored stiff, I had nothing to do. I decided to lie around on my couch and remain in that reclined position until Jesus returned.

> *Enthusiasm finds the opportunities and energy makes the most of them.*
>
> —HENRY HOSKINS

Just then the phone rang. It was a friend of mine. "Hey, Wayne!" He sounded pretty perky. "Guess what? I just got a free round of golf for two at this beautiful golf course. Only thing is, we need one more player. The tee time is in one hour. Can you go?"

All of a sudden, strength and energy surged through my soul. I snapped to attention. "You bet, I'll be there!" I almost shouted. "One hour? No problem, I'll meet you there *pronto!*"

Only one minute prior to the phone call, I had been bored stiff with nothing to look forward to. Yet once I had made a decision to do something, energy was there in an instant.

That's just the way life is, isn't it? Sometimes we think we have no strength available to us. We've got nothing left. We're done, tired and surrendered to defeat. However, that is usually the result of *indecision!* Once we make a decision to rebuild, all of a sudden we have an uncanny strength. If we don't make the decision, we'll remain drained and listless.

Step 1 in rebuilding is absolutely critical. It gets you started. Make your ever-important decision to rebuild, and then do something about it.

Step 2: Choose to Go First

Many times our lives come crashing down because relationships have been broken. Whether it's through our fault or theirs, we find ourselves living beneath the rubble. The second key to rebuilding is to make the choice to go first:

> Come to terms quickly with your enemy before it is too late (Matt. 5:25, *NLT*).

One of the things my family does is watch the Nature Channel or Discovery Network. I'm not too big on TV, but we do love animals. If you walk into our home and the TV is on, more than likely you'll find us focused on the latest findings about the African warthog, canine hygiene or equine surgery. We're funny like that, but it's clean, wholesome television. Plus the animals kind of remind me of my kids.

One of the most memorable programs I watched was about mountain rams. The deep-voiced narrator (usually with a touch of an accent) was listing the animal's biographical details with his usual zeal. There for our viewing pleasure were these husky rams boasting huge curled horns that resembled kingly crowns.

As the narrator calmly continued, the rams suddenly rammed each other. It was head-to-head combat; they were literally butting heads and locking horns. Our family sat there bug-eyed, glued to this violent development in the storyline.

An eye for an eye only ends up making the whole world blind.

—MAHATMA GHANDI

The mighty rams continued jousting with deadly determination. After a few minutes, however, we realized they were no longer locking horns. They actually were locked to one another *by* their horns; they were stuck. Any further action on either ram's part was simply a desperate attempt to be freed from the locked position. The narrator informed us that sometimes these rams can stay locked in this futile dilemma for hours, even days. Sometimes they can even die that way. What began as a contest of wills escalated into a prolonged entrapment that would only bring about further pain and quite possibly death.

The not-so-funny thing is that we humans do the same thing. We lock horns with others, and then our horns lock us. We imprison ourselves by our own angry antics, and we find ourselves locked in the same, futile position for months. We can hardly remember what the argument was even about. Slowly, the relationship dies.

Simple Wisdom from the Past

How can we avoid this fatal matchup of wills? Proverbs says something that may sound archaic in its method, but it still holds wonderful wisdom for today:

The cast lot puts an end to strife and decides between the mighty (18:18).

In the Old Testament, when two people locked horns about something, and it came to a stalemate, they settled the score in a simple way. They would say, "Stop! Wait a minute! Our relationship is dying because we have locked horns in this contest of wills. We don't know who is right or wrong, so do you know what we're going to do? We're going to repair this relationship once and for all."

Then they would take a single die and roll it. They would say, "Alright, since we can't figure out who is right or wrong, then whoever rolls the higher number is right and the one who rolls the lower is wrong. Agreed?"

"Agreed. Then we can get on with life!"

Let's say one rolled a five and the other rolled a two.

"Okay! It turns out that you were right and I was wrong. Please allow me to apologize. I'm sorry," the individual who rolled a two would say.

"You're forgiven."

"Now, let's rebuild that friendship!"

> *There are usually two sides to every argument but no end.*
>
> —ANONYMOUS

Sound outdated? With today's advanced, technological civilization, we would say this is obsolete. Throw dice? Only people in primitive cultures would do something so ridiculous. However, do you know who is really ridiculous? We are! We're the ones who lock horns and battle for years until we finally end up dying before the relationship is ever rebuilt.

Let me finish that nature show for you. When one of the rams finally died, the living ram's horns were still locked on to the dead body. The living ram had to drag the carcass around until it was dislodged.

I wonder, *How many dead bodies do we have locked in our horns? How many dead relationships are we dragging around, waiting for them to fall off? Have you ever locked horns with someone, resulting in the death of that relationship?*

God tells us to cast a lot and get back to rebuilding our relationships before they die.

First and Foremost

Humble yourself and go first. That's what Jesus did. He was hanging on the cross because of the sins of the people. Jesus took the consequences of those sins upon Himself in order that you could be free to rebuild your relationship with God. That was His mission. Jesus took the initiative and went first.

Forgiveness is the oil of relationships.

—JOSH MCDOWELL

As Christians, we might protest, "Wait a minute! It wasn't Your fault, Jesus. They should have been the ones to say, 'Please forgive me. I am sorry.' You should have waited for them, and *then* You could have said, 'I forgive.'"

Yes, this makes complete sense, but if Jesus had waited, we might still be dead in our sin. He might never have been able to restore our relationship with God. Instead, Jesus said, "Why wait? I'll go first and usher in redemption. Why not go first when it comes to healing?"

Arlene's Story

Arlene and I went to Bible college together. She was about 27 years old and single. I noticed some small, microscopic plastic-surgery lines on her face. One day, curiosity got the best of me. I asked, "Arlene, how did you get those little marks all over your face and neck?"

She said, "You really want to know?"

She began to tell me her story: "I married early. I was a Christian, but I married someone who wasn't. He also had a drinking problem I chose to overlook. I soon found out that whenever he got drunk, a rage would come out of him like none I had ever known. He started by just picking arguments with me. Then he began punching the walls next to my head in order to frighten me.

"About two years after we were married, he got drunk one night and came home while I was sleeping. He began to trash the house in his drunken stupor. He broke mirrors, lamps, tables and chairs—anything he could find. He was in a terrible rage.

"When I ran downstairs to try to stop him, he pulled out a knife from the kitchen drawer and stabbed me 28 times. He left me for dead in a pool of blood and jumped in the car and took off.

"Before I went unconscious, the neighbors had heard my screams and called the emergency room. The paramedics arrived shortly and were able to save my life. I spent the next year and a half in the hospital undergoing multiple reconstructive surgeries and hours of therapy."

When she finished telling me her story, she stopped and looked at me with clear, bright eyes.

Flabbergasted, I said, "Didn't you get mad? I mean, what ever happened to him? Don't you want revenge?"

"No," she said. She told me he had been caught and was serving time in prison, but she had moved on with her life. He still claims it was the alcohol at fault and not him.

I couldn't believe it. "Has he ever asked you for forgiveness?"

"No," she said.

Still unconvinced, I continued, "Still, you forgave him?"

"Yep."

"But," I said, "how in the world could you do that?"

She told me, "Somebody had to go first. It might as well be me. Why wait for him? He took from me one night of my life, and I can't afford to give him one more second. God has an assignment for me to accomplish, and I have only one life to give for my master. I don't have a minute to lose to yesterday's calamities."

The weak can never forgive. Forgiveness is the attribute of the strong.

—MAHATMA GHANDI

She was studying to be a missionary in order to bring the good news to people she had never met before.

I learned a valuable lesson from this dear lady, one that has lasted a lifetime. I learned that in life the key to rebuilding your life above the rubble is making a decision to go first. Don't drag around dead relationships or hurts from the past. Take the initiative to repair. Go first. It will free you from frustration, and you'll be able to live your own life to the fullest.

Step 3: Rebuild According to God's Word and Ways

If you want Bible blessings, you need to do it the Bible way! When you come out of a destroyed relationship, be sure to get it right and rebuild according to God's Word and God's ways. Otherwise, as the old lyric goes, you'll find "the second verse, same as the first."

I ruined a few relationships before I came to know Jesus. I was living with a girl in my late teens. Five days before we were to be married, we got into a fight and canceled the wedding.

Soon after that, I surrendered my life to Christ and became a Christian. Then I met my wife-to-be, Anna, in Bible college, and we started dating. But have you ever noticed your hormones don't get converted? I wish they would, but they don't. I had the same hormones I had always had before I knew the Lord, and they were raging through my "new creation" body.

I could be sitting next to Anna in the park and my hormones would start to boil. I could feel it. My eyes would start rapidly blinking, *boink, boink, boink!* I'd start to feel as if I would faint right there. (It might have been better that way.) I'd begin sweating and twitching, and my hormones would start to morph me into a hideous creature.

> *We must accept finite disappointment but never lose infinite hope.*
>
> —DR. MARTIN LUTHER KING, JR.

I knew that if I didn't build correctly from the very beginning, I would blow it all over again with this precious girl. I knew all too well that my past track record wasn't very promising—I had been kicked out of two schools and had to finish high school through a correspondence course. I had even left home to join a rock-and-roll group.

I said to Anna, "You know I come from a bad past, and I've had some bad relationships along the way. We both know that Scripture says, 'Unless the LORD builds the house, they labor in vain who build it' [Ps. 127:1]. So let's allow the Lord to build our relationship. Let's keep each other accountable to build our relationship God's way, and let's not allow anything to distract us from that."

She agreed.

Anna and I actually made a covenant. We promised together that if we were going to build, then we had to do it right. Our covenant bound us to build our relationship according to God's Word and His righteous ways. One of the stipulations of our covenant was that we would refrain from physical contact. In fact, we decided that if we were ever going to "park," it would be in her parents' driveway so that they could keep an eye on us. Every once and again, we would see the blinds open just a bit and a curious parental eyeball appear. We would talk for hours sitting in her parents' driveway.

Now we can look back on it and laugh. Yet after 30 years of marriage, if I had to do it all over again, I would do it exactly the same. Why? Because it allowed us to build our relationship God's way! It's a structure that has stood the test of time.

A Daily Word with God

Rebuilding God's way is impossible without an owner's manual. That's why God gave us the Bible. Someone once said that the word "Bible" is an acronym that stands for "Basic Instructions Before Leaving Earth."

Back when Anna and I were dating, I was just learning about God, so I had to cling to His Word and His righteousness to remain pure and true. It was my only hope.

> I am completely discouraged—I lie in the dust. Revive me by your Word. I cling to your commands and follow them as closely as I can. Lord, don't let me make a mess of things. If you will only help me to want your will, then I will follow your laws even more closely (Ps. 119:25,30-32, *TLB*).

When you're lying in the dust, your life decimated by your own doing or the doing of someone else, there's one hope: God's Word. Scripture reminds us that if we cling closely to God's commands, He can help us to accomplish His will.

Success Means to Constantly Rebuild

The best way to rebuild is according to God's design. You will never regret it. When you come out of a bad past or a bad situation, the

Lord will take you right where you are and start His rebuilding process. Remember the three nonnegotiable rebuilding steps:

1. Make a decision to rebuild.
2. Choose to go first.
3. Rebuild according to God's Word and His ways.

There is no other way. So why not go for it!

> *Things which eye has not seen and ear has not heard,*
> *and which have not entered the heart of man, all that*
> *God has prepared for those who love Him.*
>
> 1 Corinthians 2:9

DEVELOPING A LIFE OF EXCELLENCE

Many people come to church feeling like yesterday's newspaper—thrown aside and useless. They're no longer a neat, fresh copy with attractive pictures and attention-grabbing headlines. Like issues found at the bottom of the pile, they have struggles and hurts, which have left them feeling a little wrinkled and outdated.

Life in the Vise

Years ago, one of America's first nuclear submarines was being tested to determine her capacity to withstand the pressures of the deep ocean. Scientists, scholars and military stars were excited to test the seaworthiness of the newest, best and most expensive submarine ever. It was the last, most critical step in what would become a powerful addition to the country's military defense.

The test sub was the USS *Thresher*. The day of the launch was a star-studded event. As many watched from above, the sub was slowly lowered and softly submerged into the cobalt depths. The anticipation was high. Every precaution had been taken—every test available had been completed precisely, and all reassurances were in place. The sub also was connected by sonar and radio in order to keep it in constant communication with the mother ship on the ocean's surface.

The sub began to dive, reaching depths never before attained by any submarine in history. The military brass cheered as each new record depth was logged. But all of a sudden, the surface ship lost all contact with the *Thresher*. Desperate attempts to reestablish communication proved futile. First, garbled transmissions were barely made out. Then, listeners reported a sound "like air rushing into an air tank." Finally, there was silence. This eerie disconnection began to feel like Houdini's disappearing act, leaving its captive audience stumped and fearing the worst.

A deep-sea research vessel was quickly deployed to the spot where contact with the *Thresher* had been lost. Arriving at the scene, the vessel communicated a ghostly discovery. Twisted pieces of debris from the once high-powered submarine were strewn haplessly over the ocean floor. It looked as if giant hands had, in a fit of anger, shredded her like an old newspaper.

After months of fact-finding and evidence gathering, the military delivered its conclusion: The welding on one of the bulkheads had given way due to the intense pressure of the depths. The strain weakened the sub, causing her to instantly implode like a neon light shattering. Her bulk and 129-man crew lay across 400 square yards of the ocean bottom.

Negative Air Pressure

When the pressure on the outside is greater than the pressure on the inside, it is called negative air pressure. The opposite is called positive air pressure. Negative air pressure leads to events like the tragedy aboard the USS *Thresher*, an event still commemorated as a terrible loss. A high-powered, best-of-the-best masterpiece of modern technology had been undermined by one crack. That tiny crack had caused the vessel to implode, allowing an entire sea to break in.

That same tragedy can strike our lives, too. It happens when we allow negative pressure to crack our armor and shred our hearts. Before we realize it, a tiny crack leads to our lives imploding from the outside in.

Then inadvertent comments and errant questions flood through the rubble of our lives, reminding us of what we've tried so hard to forget. The shattered remains of our broken hearts bear sharp edges that continue to dig in with cutting accuracy. It's not long before we collapse under the pressure of what we have not become or what we have not achieved.

Aim at heaven and you will get earth thrown in. Aim at earth and you will get neither.

—C. S. LEWIS

Although we hate ourselves for doing it, we allow ourselves to be squeezed into other people's perceptions of us. Even though the broken expectations are lies, we begin to believe them and think, *Well, I guess this is just the way I'm supposed to live.* We shrug, sigh and settle for living a life beneath our potential.

Don't let the world around you squeeze you into its own mould, but let God re-make you so that your whole attitude of mind is changed. Thus you will prove in practice that the will of God is good (Rom. 12:2, *Phillips*).

Positive Air Pressure

Having Christ in your heart is not simply a badge indicating that you're a Christian. It is far more than that! Christ fills you with His presence so that you will not have to be squeezed into the world's mold—succumbing to what others think or falling victim to your own faulty conclusions.

First John 4:4 assures us, "Greater is He who is in you than he who is in the world." When you are in the depths, don't give in. Jesus won't. His presence will give you the confidence and strength to press through:

I will never fail you. I will never forsake you (Heb. 13:5, *NLT*).

Off and Running

Realizing God's presence in your life and gaining the confidence to rebuild are only the beginning. Now comes the most important part: applying them. Just because you and I come out of the blocks well doesn't exempt us from running the race. You must now embark on the journey to regain what God had planned for you in the first place.

Salvation is not arrival. It is admission. It doesn't mean that once you say yes to Jesus you can dial in the cruise control, relax and fall back into your old lifestyle. Rather, you are gaining admittance into God's perfecting program for wayward kids.

Don't miss this: God graciously embarks you upon a lifetime of restoration. He begins to restore you and your life to the original masterpiece He first designed, and that takes time. It is like restoring an old car—bringing it back to its original design. It takes a hobbyist time, careful effort and a lot of love to gingerly restore each part. That's exactly what God does when He restores you, your marriage, your faith, your hope and your dreams. Little by little, layer by layer, He restores each part of your life. He removes the damaged parts and the worn items, and He sands away the rust spots so that He can apply a new coat of paint.

Hope is a waking dream.

—ARISTOTLE

It is precisely at this point that we need to have a willingness to cooperate with what God is doing, step by painstaking step. Sometimes the sanding and the scraping are not things I look forward to, but the restoration process requires those kinds of refining.

"I will refine them like silver and test them like gold. They will call on my name and I will answer them; I will say, 'They are my people,' and they will say, 'The LORD is our God'"* (Zech. 13:9, *NIV*, emphasis added).

Masterpieces in the Making

One of the great artists who resides in Hawaii is a talented conservationist named John Wyland. He is well known for his whale murals that span the sides of vast walls and even skyscrapers.

I visited one of his galleries and was in awe of his sculptures, paintings and creations of art. There was no piece that didn't enrapture my heart. I loved them all. His attention to detail and color made everything absolutely outstanding in quality and creativity.

If you were to infinitely multiply my awe of Wyland's work, you would just begin to approach the entry level of our creator's magnificence and splendor. God makes no junk. And the fact that God chose to create you lets you in on a little secret: *You are infinitely valuable, for within you resides divine potential.*

God's Names

O LORD our Lord, how excellent is thy name (Ps. 8:1, *KJV*).

The names of God always depict His character. They define who He is. When the Bible describes God as *Jehovah Rapha* (the God who heals), it tells us that it is God's very nature to heal. Whatever He touches is restored and made new. Therefore, when Scripture instructs us that God's name is excellent, it means that God is an excellent God. His very nature is the essence of excellence, and whatever He creates is created for excellence.

> *God created us in His image, and He is a great God! Therefore, God intended us to be great!*

Now, if God created us in His image, then it must be God's desire that we be an excellent people. It's also His continuing desire for each of us to have a life of excellence. He doesn't want us to settle for mediocrity. His master plan for our lives is excellence.

Some people say, "Wayne, that's hard. I'm just not there yet, you know? I don't think I'll ever be excellent in my marriage, my thoughts or my life. Does that make me a lost cause?

Am I disqualified from running this race?"

The Process of Excellence

Excellence is not necessarily defined as a state of being or a position arrived at. Let's look to Solomon's legacy to discover something about God's process:

> A wise man will hear and *increase* in learning (Prov. 1:5, emphasis added).

God says a wise person is defined as one who is increasing. Wisdom is a process, a lifestyle, an ongoing way of living. He doesn't say wisdom (or excellence) happens when you arrive at a predetermined level. Rather, a wise person will always be hearing and increasing in learning.

The future belongs to those who believe in their dreams.

—ELEANOR ROOSEVELT

God tells us that we can be wise even if we are only in elementary school! We find in Luke 2:46-47 that Jesus Himself was found, at age 12, in the Temple "sitting among the religious teachers, discussing deep questions with them. And all who heard him were amazed at his understanding and his answers" (*NLT*). He was just a preteen, but still Jesus amazed the best theologians in the land.

A heart of wisdom is found not in someone who has "arrived" as much as in someone who is *learning along the way.* That is what wholeness is all about. We are not perfect people, but we are a people who choose to enter His perfecting process. People who choose this process will have lives marked by a consistent increase in understanding, learning and depth. It is a *process*:

> But we . . . are being transformed into the same image from glory to glory, just as from the Lord, the Spirit (2 Cor. 3:18).

We grow from "glory to glory" through a *process* of "being transformed." If the process is in motion, wisdom is flowing and likeness to the Lord is increasing. That is the goal. That is how the restoration process works best. Therefore, in the words of one of our nation's heroes, "Let's roll!"

There are three simple steps that will challenge us to be all God created us to be. Let's look at a blueprint for developing a life of excellence.

Step 1: Don't Be Afraid to Dream

> It will come about after this that I will pour out My Spirit on all mankind; and your sons and daughters will prophesy, your old men will dream dreams, your young men will see visions (Joel 2:28).

In this day and age, many people have stopped dreaming. We've lost vision for what our futures could hold. Our dreams for our marriages, our jobs and our lives have become blurred. Marred by past mistakes and broken expectations, the "dreamer" inside of us no longer believes.

We settle for a discounted marriage, a half-priced family and a secondhand future. We've caved in to the dictates of our world and resigned ourselves to living lives of quiet discontent.

Yet our dreams are vitally important to our realizing God's vision for the potential of our lives.

Hold fast to dreams
For if dreams die
Life is a broken-winged bird
That cannot fly.
Hold fast to your dreams
For when dreams go
Life is a barren field
Frozen with snow.

—LANGSTON HUGHES

When God tells us, "Old men will dream dreams," He is not giving us a chronological prerequisite or an age-sensitive promise. You don't have to wait until your hair and teeth fall out before you can dream. The Lord is simply saying: It's never too late to start to dream again!

God knew we were going to stop dreaming in these last days, so He is pouring forth His Spirit in a new way to help us dream again. We must not be afraid to dream. He is going to help us do it.

Never underestimate the power of a dream in transforming a life!

"I Have a Dream!"

No one can deny how one dream forever altered the landscape of America. Its realization was nowhere seen more poignantly than on the steps of the Lincoln Memorial on August 28, 1963.

In the hot noonday sun, Nobel Peace Prize recipient Martin Luther King, Jr., passionately spoke out to the dream-starved masses:

> I say to you today my friends so even though we face the difficulties of today and tomorrow, *I still have a dream.* . . .
> *I have a dream* that one day this nation will rise up and live out the true meaning of its creed: "We hold these truths to be self-evident, that all men are created equal." . . . *I have*

a dream that my four little children will one day live in a nation where they will not be judged by the color of their skin but by the content of their character. *I have a dream today.*[1]

That dream rang all across America, inspiring the more than 250,000 people gathered near the Lincoln Memorial and leading to events like the march from Selma. That solitary dream also fueled picketers in Birmingham. They had their houses burned, their cars thrashed and their children scorned, but their stubborn dreams refused defeat. One man's dream changed the course of America's history!

Look at what God did through 12 ragtag ruffians from Galilee. They began as everyday fishermen, farmers and feisty brothers. Yet within three and a half years, they changed the world, history and even eternity!

Never underestimate the compelling power of a dream.

Even as God placed one dream in the heart of Martin Luther King, Jr., He also has placed a dream in your heart. Just imagine if all our dreams began to fly. Do you understand how we could change our families, our churches and our world?

Dreams Make Life Worth Living

It was the grand opening of the magnificent Walt Disney World complex in Orlando, Florida. Walt Disney's widow, Lillian Disney, was in attendance at the dedication, and the architect of the entertainment megacomplex stood next to her. He scanned the vast enterprise and said, "Wow! Mrs. Disney, I wish Walt could have seen this."

She turned to the architect and said, "He did! That's why it's here."

First, think. Second, believe. Third, dream. And finally, dare.

—WALT DISNEY

Nothing happens until someone starts to dream, so don't stop dreaming. Your dream may take a lifetime to achieve, but it will give you direction, hope and the stamina to rise above setbacks. It will be used by God to refine your character, increase your relational skills and develop what you thought you could not.

God knows the power of vision. He knows vision propels people to their best and elevates them to live life above the rubble. God knows without vision and without dreams, people die: "Where there is no vision, the people perish" (Prov. 29:18, KJV).

How are you stewarding the dream God has placed in your heart? Are you ignoring it? Have you abandoned it? Instead, take some time to fan the flames afresh. It is for this very reason that the Holy Spirit is being poured out on God's people in these last days. It's time to dream again!

And afterward, I will pour out my Spirit on all people. Your sons and daughters will prophesy, your old men will dream dreams, your young men will see visions (Joel 2:28, NIV).

It Is Time to Dream God-Sized Dreams

"Dream no small dreams for they have no power to move the hearts of men."[2]

Don't be afraid to dream, even though your dream may be beyond your reach. If your dream is more of a personal desire than a God-authored assignment, He will let you know. A dream isn't an abstract, wish-upon-a-star fantasy that only serves to inflate your ego. Rather, God encourages dreams that honor Him and help the people He loves.

Be ready to amend and adjust your sights to match His, but you have to start somewhere. In other words, it's difficult to steer a parked car, but if you get it rolling in the right direction, you can make adjustments along the way.

Here are a few basics guidelines for dreams:

- **Dreams are God glorifying and people helping.**
  God-sized dreams always represent God's heart. They are not about me. Remember that God doesn't exist for my purposes. I exist for His!
- **Dreams do not demand credit or my name in lights.**
  I am content to allow God alone to receive the credit.

> *We judge of man's wisdom by his hope.*
>
> —RALPH WALDO EMERSON

Dreams can either create prima donnas or proven servants. I am content to have been granted the privilege to *serve*, not to be acknowledged.

- **Dreams require me to develop my character and competence in order for them to be fulfilled.**
  Simply because I have dreams does not mean that I am mature enough to receive them. David was anointed king of Israel in 1 Samuel 16, but it wasn't until 17 chapters later that he actually took the throne. There were lessons to be learned, character to be built, tears to be shed and endurance to be developed. God-sized dreams require God-sized development.
- **Dreams necessitate counsel, evaluation and adjustments along the way.**
  Don't ever let dreams become "God told me" or justifications for being unaccountable. Even the apostle Paul submitted his views to those God put in authority over him. It was the only way to make sure that he was not

"running . . . in vain" (Gal. 2:2).

· **Dreams ultimately bring others closer to God.**
God-sized dreams have one ultimate goal: not to promote
my own causes but to introduce others to the Father. John
the Baptist said, "He must increase, but I must decrease"
(John 3:30).

· **Dreams require me to start with what I already have.**
God-sized dreams don't come preassembled. They come
in kit form. I start with what I have. If God sees me as
faithful with even a little, then He will add more. If I am
not faithful with what I already have, why should He
give me what I don't yet have?

God Dreams, Too!

Now glory be to God who by his mighty power at work
within us is *able to do far more than we would ever dare to ask or
even dream of*—infinitely beyond our highest prayers, desires,
thoughts, or hopes (Eph. 3:20, *TLB*, emphasis added).

By His power in you, God can do things far beyond anything you
can conceive, even for yourself. What that tells you is that God
wants you to dream the best
dream possible for your life. If
you are married, dream the greatest dream you possibly can for
your marriage and your family.
If you are a single person, dream
a great dream for your future. If
you are in ministry, dream the
biggest, most God-sized dream
you can possibly dream. Why? Because He can exceed even your
dream! Start by praying this prayer:

*You cannot depend
on your eyes when
your imagination
is out of focus.*

—MARK TWAIN

God, how can You use me? God, dream Your biggest,
best dream for my life. Give me Your dream because
You promised to do so. Amen.

Then begin to ponder the questions: What can God do through me? What would I really love doing for God that would make it feel like Christmas every day?

Finally, stop, pray, and wait for God's answer. When you do, God will be faithful to give you a vision of what He can do through you. When you've received it, He'll ask, "Are you ready?"

You'll reply, "Yes!"

God will then say, "My dreams for you are bigger still!"

God can and does exceed abundantly above all we ask or even dream of—so dream big. Why? Because His dreams are bigger still! In fact, He may be saying to you and me that the only way we'll even get close to His plans for our lives is to dream big dreams.

God is not concerned that we will dream too big. He is more concerned that we will settle for far too little.

Step 2: Be Willing to Pay the Price

For the dream comes through much effort (Eccles. 5:3).

Here's the part we don't like to hear: Dreams fulfilled come at a price. That's right. Salvation is free. Everything else costs!

If you want a good marriage, it will cost you something. It will cost you self-control, kindness, learning how to be still, learning how to forgive and asking for help when your pride would rather deny that the need for help even exists.

If you want a good business, it will cost. If you want a life of character and integrity, it will cost. If you have a dream, it will come at a price.

What is the price you pay for capturing God's dreams in your life? Nothing less than your willingness to build the depth of character that is required to sustain the weight of that dream. You see, a small, inconsequential dream may not require much, but God-sized ones require God-sized character. *When you dream God-sized dreams, you don't necessarily make the dream; rather, it begins to make you.*

> *Yes, you can be a dreamer and a doer too, if you will remove one word from your vocabulary: impossible.*
>
> —ROBERT SCHULLER

The Price of Character

Character doesn't come cheap. It comes at a price—the price of digging your knees into the carpet, the price of studying, the price of suffering and the price of going through trials and discipline. Yet we *must* be willing to pay the price:

> Everything else is worthless when compared with the priceless gain of knowing Christ Jesus my Lord. So, *whatever it takes,* I will be one who lives in the fresh newness of life (Phil. 3:8,11, *TLB*, emphasis added).

Circle those three words, "whatever it takes," and inscribe them on your heart. Have a whatever-it-takes heart and mindset. Whatever it takes, be willing to pay the price for character. And whatever it takes, be counted among those who live in the newness of life.

Some people say, "But, Wayne, I see people who don't serve God, but they get all kinds of stuff. They get accolades, money, prestige and promotion—and they're not even serving God! They even sin and get rewarded. What about that?"

The wisest king of all time, King Solomon, said:

Though a man sins a hundred times and still lives,
I know very well that those who fear God will be better
off (Eccles. 8:12, *TLB*).

In other words, don't do it that way. Play according to God's rules. King Solomon had done it all. He had even engaged in all kinds of iniquities, but he knew better than anyone else that sin doesn't pay. There's nothing better than following God. Do whatever it takes to follow Him and develop character.

When we become aware that we do not have to escape our pains . . . those very pains are transformed from expressions of despair into signs of hope.

—HENRI J. M. NOUWEN

Here are three "willing" attitudes we need to exercise to fulfill God's dreams for our lives. Let's consider these as we strive to do whatever it takes:

1. Be willing to experience suffering.

All discipline for the moment seems not to be joyful, but sorrowful; yet to those who have been trained by it, afterwards it yields the peaceful fruit of righteousness (Heb. 12:11).

Be willing to experience suffering for the sake of spiritual growth. Maturity is not a painless process, but the aches can be greatly reduced when you know what it will produce!

Godly suffering means telling your flesh to be quiet when God is talking to you. This means tithing when you'd rather keep the money for yourself. This means not giving audience to lewd thoughts, which lure you into virtual escapades in your mind. This means smiling and remaining cordial when you'd rather rearrange someone's teeth.

> This suffering is all part of the work God has given you. Christ, who suffered for you, is your example. Follow in his steps (1 Pet. 2:21, *TLB*).

Suffering for the sake of spiritual growth is something that Jesus did. As we follow Him and His example, we'll find that sometimes along the way, achieving a God-sized dream requires suffering. Why? Because it forges a strength of character. Be willing to suffer for the sake of spiritual growth and don't give up!

We shall draw from the heart of suffering itself the means of inspiration and survival.

—WINSTON CHURCHILL

2. Be willing to break through quitting points. Every one of us has quitting points. This is where someone tests your patience to a certain limit and you say, "That's it!" Then you give up and quit. That point is your predetermined, automatic quitting point.

What are some of your quitting points?

All of us have quitting points. Maybe it's when someone gives us trouble or doesn't accept our suggestions. Maybe it's when things don't go exactly the way we want. Maybe it's when our children refuse to listen for the fifth time, so we write them off in our minds and hearts. We've quit on them because their immaturity or inattentiveness has met our quitting points.

Always remember that the measure of a man or a woman is determined by what it takes to derail his or her commitments to marriage, to faith, to a friendship or to a church home. *What is your quitting point?* Be very mindful of this so that you can safeguard your heart.

Who knows what your quitting points are? Who's been keeping a watchful eye and recording every bail-out point? Actually, someone has been keeping careful track and recording each weakness with insolent purpose. Who? The devil.

He keeps tally of all of your quitting points. He watches you carefully and knows that if you bail out at a certain level of pain, then he's got you pegged. Like a military opponent plotting the coordinates of a submarine he plans to intercept, so too the adversary of our souls keeps track of how much you can handle. He knows at what precise point on the pain meter you will bail out.

When he ascertains your quitting points and sees that you are unwilling to change, he starts his insidious mission. If he wants to steer your life, all he has to do is increase the cost in a relationship and you will bail out. He will increase the pain in your life and you will quietly excuse yourself. He will increase the commitment in your ministry and you will quit.

Without our willingness to break through quitting points, he can and will commandeer your future. Just like an alien space pirate taking over the starship *Enterprise*, he will pilot and maneuver your life. How? He knows precisely at what point you are going to bail out.

> *Most people give up just when they're about to achieve success. They quit on the one-yard line. They give up at the last minute of the game one foot from a winning touchdown.*
>
> —H. ROSS PEROT

Instead, the Bible says that if God has called you to a certain commitment, then press through those quitting points. You must be willing to persevere to God's best. Break through and keep going in God's direction. It's the only way:

He conquers who endures.

—PERSIUS

For you have need of *endurance*, so that when you have done the will of God, you may receive what was promised (Heb. 10:36, emphasis added).

Circle the word "endurance" in your heart and mind, because you need to practice improving your endurance. By doing so, you'll defy the devil and his plot to take you down. You'll begin to break through to God's next level for your life.

3. Be willing to raise the bar of excellence for the sake of the kingdom of God.

A dull axe requires great strength; be wise and sharpen the blade (Eccles. 10:10, *TLB*).

Continue to sharpen yourself and raise the bar of excellence in your life. Bring out the best in yourself. Read Paul's encouragement:

We request and exhort you in the Lord Jesus, that as you received from us instruction as to how you ought to walk and please God (just as you actually do walk), *that you excel still more* (1 Thess. 4:1, emphasis added).

Did you catch that? "Excel still more"? Paul urges you to keep on improving for the sake of the kingdom of God. Be willing to keep improving, and do so diligently every single day. Look for something to improve about yourself. It may be the way you comb your hair or the way you look people in the eye. It may be the way you shake hands or something about your posture or speech. Instead of responding to requests by muttering, "Yeah, okay," say with zeal, "Sure, I would love to!" When someone asks for your help, instead of replying, "Well, I guess," say, "I would be more than honored to help!"

> *We are what we repeatedly do. Excellence, then is not an act, but a habit.*
>
> —ARISTOTLE

Where can you improve? Perhaps it's in your discipline, the way you treat your spouse or the way you share your faith with others. Do something to excel still more for the sake of the Kingdom. Improve yourself 1 percent a day for one year and see how much you grow. Raise the bar!

Inch by Inch, It's a Cinch

I played club soccer at the University of Oregon where our scrimmage field happened to be in the middle of a practice track. All around us, various teams would be practicing the high jump, pole vault, triple jump and other events. (Incidentally, Eugene, Oregon, is a mecca for track and field. In fact, that's where Nike got its start.) It was on that selfsame track that I learned an amazing life lesson.

I remember being intrigued by a persistent high jumper. One day, he was practicing for a prestigious track meet that was eight months away. The bar on the high jump was set at 5'9". Now, 5'9" is taller than I am, so for me that is high. He made his attempt and cleared the bar. I looked at him and thought, *Wow! That's amazing! No springs, no pogo stick. He just jumped!* If I ever cleared the bar at 5'9", I would retire. I would take a picture of myself next to the bar, buy myself the biggest trophy I could afford and brag endlessly to my kids. Not this athlete. Instead of retiring, he raised the bar and jumped again. He jumped 5'10", and instead of being satisfied, he raised the bar again. He did this for eight months.

> *Hold yourself to a higher standard than anybody expects of you. Never excuse yourself.*
>
> —HENRY WARD BEECHER

Finally, the day of the track meet arrived. I bought a ticket for the event just to watch the high jumper. The stadium was packed when the high jump competition began. Many of the high jumpers faulted early, failing to clear the bar at 6'1" and 6'2". Finally, the bar was set at 6'4". My high jumper was the final contestant. He would be given three chances to clear 6'4", and if he did, he would win.

He set out on his first attempt, but he hit the bar, falling to the ground with the bar in tow. On his second attempt, he again dislodged the bar. The crowd grew nervous with anticipation as he faced his third, and final, attempt. I can still recall his consulting with his coach, probably about the thrust of his head, the arch of his back or the timing of his foot. When he had mentally gone through each step and every maneuver, he returned to the field. He stared at the bar as if he were striking a deal with it.

After what seemed like an eternity, the young man nodded slightly and started his long, semicircular run toward the bar. With every ounce of his conditioned strength and power, he planted one foot into the ground and launched into his final jump. Every tendon and joint stretched tight as he catapulted his body into the air. He thrust his head toward the clouds, his back arched in a precise curve over the top of the bar. His foot flicked at the precise moment, and he began his descent. *He had cleared the bar!*

His teammates rushed out of the grandstands cheering. Caught up in the emotion of the moment, I found myself crying and running toward the champion saying, "You don't even know me, but I want to give you a hug!" His feat was amazing to me. I remembered his attempting to clear 5'9". Yet all the while, he had the potential to clear 6'4".

Now let me ask you a question: What brought out his potential to clear the bar at 6'4"? He would never have realized that potential within himself unless he had first been willing to raise the bar.

Some of us today are jumping at 2'6" in our daily lives. We figure that's good enough. But God says, "Inside of you, there is the potential to clear 6'4"."

Some respond, "Not me! I'm a 2'6" kind of person." But God knows there is so much more inside of you. Much more! In order to achieve it, though, you must be willing to raise the bar.

God does not insist that we raise the bar a foot at a time. One inch is fine. This means incrementally increasing your abilities. Keep improving yourself for the sake of the kingdom of God, and the potential God has wired up inside of you will begin to emerge.

Step 3: Enjoy the Ride

Thou wilt shew me the path of life: in thy presence is fulness of joy; at thy right hand there are pleasures for evermore (Ps. 16:11, *KJV*).

There are plenty of challenges and hills to climb in this journey called life. May they never overshadow the joy of the sunsets and flowers that we experience along the way. We must make sure that regardless of our circumstances, we enjoy the ride.

There is a book of Jewish writings, the *Talmud*, which teaches that God is going to hold us accountable for all the things that He put on this earth for us to enjoy and we didn't take time to do so.

God created things for you to enjoy. Stop and enjoy them. Enjoy life. Enjoy the sunshine and enjoy the rain. When you go home, enjoy your meal. When your wife says, "Mow the lawn," enjoy mowing the lawn. Take the dog for a walk—and enjoy it. Enjoy the ride. This life is so very short to not enjoy:

> *The quality of a person's life is in direct proportion to their commitment to excellence, regardless of their chosen field of endeavor.*
>
> —VINCE LOMBARDI

The joy of the LORD is your strength (Neh. 8:10).

We limp weakly through life because we forget to pack joy in our luggage. God provides it, but we forget to take it along. We let life get us down, and joy drains out of us like a leaky inflatable swimming pool. However, like the motto of a well-known credit card reminds us, "Don't leave home without it!" In every activity we attend, we need to carry along a wonderful pack of joy. It will come in handy in more instances than we realize.

Don't Let Life Pass You By

One summer, our family went to Disneyland. One of the attractions my son wanted to check out was the Indiana Jones ride. "Let's go for it!" I said.

Now, I'm an analytical person, and I watch stuff. As we were working our way through the line, I said, "See that, Aaron? See that little creature on the rock? It's not really a creature at all. It's a mechanical device that's computer activated."

"Really?" he asked.

"Yeah! And see the shapes on the wall? They're made by a light projected through a special filter called a gobo. See it?"

"Oh, yeah!" said Aaron. "Cool."

Spurred further by his interest, I continued, "See that rock face over there, with the mist gliding across it? That's smoke coming from a machine. It's not really mist at all."

"Really?"

Excitedly, I continued to instruct my young acolyte: "And see that over there? That's a mirror making those shapes on the wall."

"Huh?" His interest in me began to fade as he anticipated the ride. We climbed into the car.

"Do you see how this jeep is painted to look old, Aaron? It's actually brand-new. Check out the serial number."

"Yeah, Dad."

"And look under the dash. There aren't any wires. Know why? Because it's on a track." I was morphing into a combination of Mr. Spock and Sherlock Holmes. The jeep suddenly lunged forward and we were in motion. The speed increased, and we whipped around a corner, eliciting screams from the car next to us.

> *God is going to hold us accountable for all the things that He put on this earth for us to enjoy and we didn't take time to do so.*
>
> —THE *TALMUD*

"That was a good effect, Aaron, but if it had been banked another 10 degrees, the g-force would have been better. It really would have made your stomach drop! What do you think, Aaron?"

"Great, Dad!" said Aaron loudly, having to shout to be heard.

"You see that, Aaron? That's another mirror!" I yelled, as we zipped down the track. By this time, however, Aaron wasn't responding to my cogent analysis of the ride. He was midflight, with his head and body being jostled, twisted and pulled with every turn of the track. "See that rock coming at us? It's on a track!" I yelled. "It'll go back and get reset for the next jeep behind us! Not very effective, huh?"

No response.

Soon the jeep came to a halt and the ride was over. "You know, Aaron, if we could have made a sharper turn on that second hairpin, it would've been even better. And if the smoke had come out sooner, we could have traveled right through it."

"Hey, Dad," Aaron stopped me with a less-than-gracious tone, "Enough!"

"What do you mean, 'enough'?" I said, slightly put off by his less-than-admiring response.

Without answering, he turned and stalked off.

"Hey, you!" I called after my ingrate son. "Come over here! I've got more things to tell you!"

He kept walking. "Enough!" he called back. "I'm not riding with you anymore!"

Happiness is to be found along the way, not at the end of the road, for then the journey is over and it is too late.

—ROBERT R. UPDEGRAFF

"Okay. I'll meet you later!" I said. Under my breath, I muttered to myself, "Dumb kid! He just doesn't listen, does he? That's his problem."

As I was walking around kicking the dirt, the Lord spoke to my heart: "You missed the whole ride, didn't you? You were so busy trying to figure everything out, you missed the ride."

I stopped short in my tracks and realized, *You know, that's right! I don't even remember the ride. I was so involved in all the little details that I missed the whole ride!*

Have you ever gotten so caught up in the details of life that before you knew it the ride was over? Have you ever gotten so caught up in the preparations for a wedding that you missed the celebration? Have you ever gotten so distracted with cleaning the house before guests arrived that you alienated your family in the process?

Too often we are short with others, blaming our families and hissing at our neighbors in times of stress. We're so involved in our businesses and careers that the kids graduate from high school and we ask, "When did this happen?"

We're like Martha who "was distracted with all her preparations" (Luke 10:40). She was so distracted that she missed the honored guest, Jesus. Can you imagine having Jesus visit your house but being so distracted with the details that you don't even get to talk with Him?

There is no duty we so much underrate as the duty of being happy. By being happy we sow anonymous benefits upon the world.

—ROBERT LOUIS STEVENSON

We miss the sunrises and sunsets because we're focused on traffic or still stuck at the office. We miss the jubilance of Easter in the rush to get dressed up, into the service, back to the buffet and on to the egg hunt. And too often we miss our children's growing up as we hustle and bustle to provide for them.

My own children have grown up so quickly. It seems like they were in diapers just a few days ago. Then all too quickly they walk across the platform with a cap and gown. The next minute they're gone, and the beauty of everyday life has vanished.

Don't miss the ride!

Discover a Future and a Hope

Instead of driving at a relentless pace, slow down. God has given you a beautiful world filled with His wonders, His people and

Himself. They are all there if you take the time to enjoy them. Pause long enough to enjoy the ride. Train yourself to see what is good. Take the time to laugh with each other. Laugh at yourself. Although there are imperfections and setbacks, you'll be surprised at how wonderful life is when you have a good attitude. You will hear God better. You will enjoy His presence. You will even be pleasantly surprised at how a new perspective will help you to attract friends, laughter, joy and success.

Now that's a life of excellence! And that will only be found not beneath but *above* the rubble.

May God bless you richly as you live a life far beyond the rubble and discover the fullness of the future He desired and created for you!

"For I know the plans that I have for you," declares the Lord, "plans for welfare and not for calamity to give you a future and a hope."

Jeremiah 29:11

Notes

1. Martin Luther King, Jr., "I Have a Dream" (speech, Lincoln Memorial, Washington, D.C., August 28, 1963) *International Information Programs, United States Department of State.* http:www.usinfo.state.gov/usa/usainfo/facts/democrac/38.htm (accessed August 11, 2004), emphasis added.
2. Johann von Goethe, quoted at *Brainy Quote.* http://www.brainyquote.com/quotes/quotes/j/johannwolf/21252.html (accessed August 11, 2004).

MORE OF THE BEST
FROM WAYNE CORDEIRO

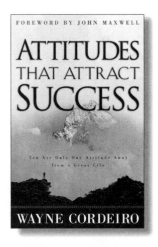
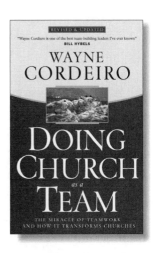

WORDS OF HOPE, HEALING AND INSPIRATION

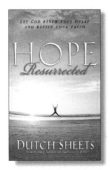

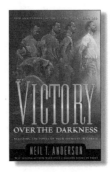

Hope Resurrected
Let God Renew Your Heart
and Revive Your Faith
Dutch Sheets
ISBN 08307.36247

Finding Hope Again
Overcoming Depression
Neil T. Anderson and
Hal Baumchen
ISBN 08307.23285

**Victory over
the Darkness**
Realizing the Power of
Your Identity in Christ
Neil T. Anderson
ISBN 08307.25644

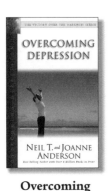

**Overcoming
Depression**
The Victory over the
Darkness Series
Neil T. Anderson and
Joanne Anderson
ISBN 08307.33515

The Dance Goes On
Despite severe disabilities,
a dancer brings readers
joy and teaches about
life, love and God.
Roberta Bandy
ISBN 08307.34082

**Suffering in
Slow Motion**
Help for the Long Journey
Through Dementia and
Other Terminal Illness
*Richard and
Pamela Kennedy*
ISBN 08307.35003